YORK NOTES

D1634764

SELECTED STORIES

CHARLES DICKENS

NOTES BY LUCY ENGLISH

Longman   York Press

The right of Lucy English to be identified as Author of this Work
has been asserted by her in accordance with the Copyright,
Designs and Patents Act 1988

YORK PRESS
322 Old Brompton Road, London SW5 9JH

PEARSON EDUCATION LIMITED
Edinburgh Gate, Harlow,
Essex CM20 2JE, United Kingdom
Associated companies, branches and representatives throughout the world

First published 2006

10 9 8 7 6 5 4 3 2 1

ISBN–10: 1–405–83560–5
ISBN–13: 978–1–405–83560–2

Illustrations by Chris Price
Phototypeset by utimestwo, Northamptonshire
Printed in China

Quotations from 'The Poor Relation's Story' are from *The New Windmill Book of Nineteenth
Century Short Stories*, edited by Mike Hamlin. Reprinted by permission of Harcourt Education.

Quotations from 'The Signalman' are from *The New Windmill Book of Mystery Stories of the
Nineteenth Century*, edited by Robert Etty. Reprinted by permission of Harcourt Education.

CONTENTS

PREFACE

York Notes are designed to give you a broader perspective on works of literature studied at GCSE and equivalent levels. With examination requirements changing in the twenty-first century, we have made a number of significant changes to this new series. We continue to help students to reach their own interpretation of the text but York Notes now have important extra-value new features.

You will discover that York Notes are genuinely interactive. The new **Checkpoint** features will make sure that you can test your knowledge and broaden your understanding. You will also be directed to excellent websites, books and films where you can follow up ideas for yourself.

The **Resources** section has been updated and an entirely new section has been devoted to how to improve your grade. Careful reading and application of the principles laid out in the Resources section guarantee improved performance.

The **Detailed summaries** include an easy-to-follow skeleton structure of the storyline, while the section on **Language and style** has been extended to offer an in-depth discussion of the writer's techniques.

The Contents page shows the structure of this study guide. However, there is no need to read from the beginning to the end as you would with a novel, play or poem. Use the Notes in the way that suits you. Our aim is to help you with your understanding of the work, not to dictate how you should learn.

Our authors are practising English teachers and examiners who have used their experience to offer a whole range of **Examiner's secrets** – useful hints to encourage exam success.

The author of these Notes is Lucy English, Head of English at George Abbot School, Guildford, and author of a number of textbooks and study guides for secondary pupils, including titles for the BBC.

The texts used in these Notes are: *A Christmas Carol*, Wordsworth Classics edition, 1993; 'The Poor Relation's Story', *New Windmill Book of Nineteenth Century Short Stories*, edited by Mike Hamlin, Heinemann, 1992, pp. 114–25; 'The Signalman', *New Windmill Book of Mystery Stories of the Nineteenth Century*, edited by Robert Etty, Heinemann, 1995, pp. 105–18.

PART ONE

INTRODUCTION

HOW TO STUDY A SHORT STORY OR NOVELLA

A short story is a prose narrative, normally designed to be read in one sitting, which tells of a specific situation, usually involving one main character. A novella is longer than a short story and introduces secondary characters and themes.

There are six features of a short story or novella:

1 THE PLOT: the plot is deliberately organised by the writer to engage the reader's attention. We often find the action moves swiftly and the plot ends suddenly at the climax of the story.

2 THE CHARACTERS: there is usually one main character in a short story and this is often the narrator. A novella tends to have more secondary characters, although these are not generally as well developed as the main characters.

3 THE VIEWPOINT/VOICE: this is who is telling the story. The viewpoint may come from the main character, a secondary character or an omniscient (all-seeing) narrator, who allows the author to show us more than the main character can see.

4 THE THEMES: these are the underlying messages, or meanings of the story. Short stories normally have one main theme or message; novellas sometimes have more.

5 THE SETTING: this concerns the time and place the author has chosen for the story. Short stories normally have a limited setting and timescale; novellas can be less restricted and have multiple settings and timescales.

6 THE LANGUAGE AND STYLE: these are the words that the author has used to influence our understanding of the short story or novella. A short story writer in particular has to be very precise with his or her choice of vocabulary.

The purpose of these York Notes is to help you understand what these stories are about and to enable you to make your own interpretations. Do not expect the study of short stories or novellas to be neat and easy: stories are chosen for examination purposes, not written for them!

 EXAMINER'S SECRET
The key to studying a short story or novella is knowing the story itself. Make sure you have read it at least three times.

AUTHOR – LIFE AND WORKS

1812 Charles John Huffam Dickens is born on 7 February in Portsmouth

1817–23 The Dickens family moves to Chatham, Kent. Dickens goes to school in 1821, but the next autumn leaves to follow his family who have moved to London

1824 Dickens is sent to work at Warren's Blacking Factory. His father is put in prison for three months for debt

1825 Dickens is allowed to leave the Blacking Factory and go to school

1827–32 The family are evicted from their house. Dickens gets a job as a solicitor's clerk and learns shorthand

1833–6 First story, 'A Dinner at Poplar Walk', is published. Reporter for the *Morning Chronicle*. Dickens marries Catherine Hogarth

1837–42 Publishes stories including *Oliver Twist*. Visits America with Catherine

1843 *A Christmas Carol* is published on 19 December

CONTEXT

1820 Death of George III. George IV becomes king

1825 First passenger railway in UK opened

1830 George IV dies. William IV becomes king

1833 Slavery abolished in British Empire

1834 The New Poor Law requires harsh workhouses to be set up in every parish

1837 William IV dies. Victoria becomes queen

1840 Victoria marries Albert

1844 Ragged Schools for poor children founded

AUTHOR – LIFE AND WORKS

CONTEXT

1847 British Factory Act restricts the hours women and children can work to ten hours a day

1848 Dickens' beloved sister, Fanny, dies

1848 Outbreak of cholera in London

1851 Great Exhibition celebrating British industry and empire held in the Crystal Palace

1852 'The Poor Relation's Story' is published at Christmas

1853 First public reading of *A Christmas Carol*

1856–8 Dickens and family move to Gad's Hill. Meets eighteen-year-old actress Ellen Ternan and starts relationship with her. Separates from Catherine

1859–65 Dickens goes on reading tours. *Great Expectations* is published. His health starts to decline. In 1865 he is involved in serious railway accident in Staplehurst, Kent

1861 Death of Prince Albert

1861–5 American Civil War

1866 'The Signalman' is published at Christmas

1866–8 Reading tours around England, Ireland and America. Health gets worse

1867 Dr Barnardo opens home for homeless children in London

1870 'Twelve Farewell Readings' given in London. He meets Queen Victoria (March). Dickens suffers a stroke on 8 June at Gad's Hill. Dies on 9 June. Buried in Westminster Abbey on 14 June

1870 First Elementary Education Act for England and Wales makes it compulsory for children aged between five and thirteen to attend school

SETTING AND BACKGROUND

INDUSTRIAL REVOLUTION

Charles Dickens was born into and lived through a time of great change. The Industrial Revolution is the term used to describe changes in working and living conditions that began in the 1760s. During this time Britain moved from being a country based around a rural and agricultural economy and lifestyle to being the world's first industrial giant. The rapid pace of the change put great strain on all levels of society. Workers were needed in large numbers for the mills and factories in the cities and there was a huge movement of people from the countryside to the new cities. Cities grew very quickly; this meant the housing available to the poor was often dreadful. The population of London grew from about 1 million in 1800 to 6 million in 1900.

The Industrial Revolution was good for many people; it gave them more money and better living conditions. However, for the poor, life was difficult. Adults and children would often work for long hours in dangerous conditions and then go home to squalor, hunger and disease.

THE RAILWAYS

The power of steam to drive factory machinery was a key element in the success of the Industrial Revolution. However, British engineers also worked out how to use it to transport people and goods long distances. This changed the way the economy worked as well as opening up new experiences to many people.

CHECK THE NET

For more information on the development and rise of the railways look at **www. railwaysarchive. co.uk.** An account of the railway accident at Staplehurst that Dickens was involved in can also be found here. Try typing 'Dickens' into the search engine.

George Stephenson opened the twenty-mile Stockton to Darlington railway in 1825 in order to carry coal. Before this horse-drawn carts would have been used. The steam engine was faster and cheaper and helped the Industrial Revolution by transporting goods more efficiently.

In 1830 the first passenger railway opened, carrying people from Liverpool to Manchester. This was very popular and caught the public imagination so much Thomas Cook organised his first 'Cook's Tour' – a day out from Leicester to Loughborough.

These new steam trains were very fast and exciting, but there were also new dangers associated with them. Dickens experienced these dangers first-hand. He was involved in a railway accident at Staplehurst in Kent in June 1865. Although he and the people he was travelling with escaped unhurt, many people died. The time he spent among the carnage influenced his writing – the train crash in 'The Signalman' is thought to be based on this experience.

POVERTY AND EDUCATION

Poverty and what to do about the poor was of real concern in Victorian England. Vast slums had built up where factory workers lived, many families sharing one tap and toilet. Conditions in these slums did not begin to improve until the 1860s when proper sewerage and drainage systems started to be installed in London.

In order to try and deal with the large numbers of poor people, the government passed the New Poor Law in 1834. This meant that any able-bodied unemployed person would only be supported if they entered the workhouse (as referred to by Scrooge in *A Christmas Carol*, Stave One, p. 17). Workhouses were made deliberately harsh environments to live and work in. Families were separated and the food was basic. It was hoped that this would discourage the 'lazy poor' from choosing to go there.

This law was disapproved of by Dickens. He wrote many stories and articles about the poor, highlighting their conditions and needs. His time working in the Blacking Factory when his family was in prison must have given him a real insight into the horrors of poverty (see section on **Charles Dickens' background**, below).

As well as highlighting the conditions of the poor, Dickens worked to provide them with relief. His friend, a wealthy lady called Angela Burdett-Coutts, provided the financial backing for many of his ideas. In the 1840s they became involved in the Ragged Schools. These schools aimed to give poor children a basic education and got their name from the ragged clothes the children wore. Dickens'

 DID YOU KNOW?

Dickens' own experiences of poverty and his desire for education influenced him when writing. *David Copperfield* is thought to be Dickens' most autobiographical work, with many events reflecting his own childhood and life. One such example is David's employment at Murdstone and Grinby's which echoes Dickens' time at the Blacking Factory.

belief that education was a route out of poverty can be seen in the two children, Ignorance and Want, who appear in *A Christmas Carol* (Stave Three, p. 74).

DICKENS AND CHRISTMAS

www. CHECK THE NET
For more information on Dickens' influence on Christmas look at **www.fidnet. com/~dap1955/ dickens** and click on 'Dickens & Christmas'.

Dickens is often credited with inventing Christmas as we know it today. His descriptions of shared family meals, turkey and stuffing, games, holly and mistletoe have become key parts of the modern Christmas. Even the Ghost of Christmas Past in *A Christmas Carol* is said to have shaped our image of Father Christmas. Perhaps the most important aspect Dickens has influenced is the idea of goodwill to all.

In the Preface to the collection of his Christmas Stories (*Christmas Books*), Dickens wrote that he intended these stories to 'awaken some loving and forbearing thoughts, never out of season in a Christian land'. This suggests that he wanted to create some sense of religious awareness as well as to keep old rituals and traditions alive. In Victorian England many people, including employers like Scrooge, did not do anything special for Christmas at all. It is possible that Dickens' stories played a part in helping to change society and its attitudes to Christmas.

Christmas celebrations appear in many of Dickens' stories and books, and after the success of *A Christmas Carol* he produced special Christmas stories for his journals (*Household Words* (1850–8) and *All the Year Round* (1859–67)). 'The Poor Relation's Story' and 'The Signalman' were both written for Christmas editions.

Perhaps the famous story about Dickens' death tells us how much he was associated with Christmas. Upon hearing of his death, a barrow girl in Covent Garden is reported to have asked, 'Then will Father Christmas die too?'

CHARLES DICKENS' BACKGROUND

www. CHECK THE NET
For more information about the life and times of Charles Dickens look at **www. dickensmuseum. com**

Charles Dickens was born in Portsmouth in 1812, the eldest son in a family of eight children. His father, John Dickens, worked as a clerk in the Navy Pay Office at Portsmouth Dockyard. When Charles was five the family moved to Chatham, Kent, another bustling naval town.

This time was a happy one for Dickens. His nurse, Mary Weller, aroused his fascination with stories and storytelling by telling him bloodthirsty tales such as 'Sweeney Todd' and 'Bluebeard'. He was not a strong child and spent much time by himself, reading and acting out stories rather than playing outside with other children. He was delighted to be sent to school in 1821, although it is not clear that he learnt much more there than his mother had earlier taught him. Dickens' pleasure in learning to read and write is recalled in *David Copperfield*.

However, life changed for the Dickens family when John Dickens was transferred to London. Charles was left in Chatham, staying with his teacher for a few months, before having to travel by himself to London to join the rest of the family who were living in a small house in Camden Town. This was the beginning of a difficult period in Dickens' life. Rather than being sent to school as he wanted, he was kept at home and given errands and tasks to do. To make matters worse, his sister, Fanny, was sent to the Royal Academy of Music, something his family couldn't really afford to do.

The family situation got worse as Dickens' father's ability to manage his money declined. They moved house and Dickens' mother tried to start a school, but with no success. Eventually, it was decided Charles had to earn money to help the family and, aged twelve, he was sent to work in a Blacking Factory. This was a factory where black dye to put on boots was made. Charles' job was to cover each pot and paste a label on it. He later wrote that this was the worst experience of his life.

Times were to get even more difficult as John Dickens was put into prison for debt. His wife and children, except Charles and Fanny, joined him there. Charles lodged with a mean-spirited old woman and had to manage his own money, something he found difficult as there was not enough for accommodation and food

CHECK THE BOOK

In *Great Expectations*, the main character, a young boy called Pip, has to travel alone from Kent to London. Look at Dickens' description of a young boy seeing London for the first time.

each week. This childhood experience never left him. It influenced much of Dickens' writing and opinions about the poor and social reform.

John Dickens was released from prison but Charles continued to work at the Blacking Factory, until his father had a falling out with the owner. When the dispute was resolved Charles' mother wanted him to return there, something Charles never forgave her for, but he was eventually allowed to go to school instead. Unfortunately, the school that was chosen was not a good one and Dickens did not enjoy his time there. He stayed here until he was fifteen when he left to start work as a solicitor's clerk.

DID YOU KNOW?

Dickens' school provided him with the basis for Salem House in *David Copperfield*.

Dickens taught himself shorthand and soon obtained a new job as a court reporter, earning a reputation for being accurate and fast. This job allowed him to see the harsh justice system in action, and shaped his opinions about society still further. Soon he moved to a new job as newspaper reporter, commenting on Parliament, London and its inhabitants. However, his interest in literature surfaced at this point and he began to write sketches and stories about London life, the first of which were published in 1833. Dickens' life as an author had begun.

Dickens continued to write, publishing under the **pseudonym** 'Boz', and life began to change for him. He earned enough money to pay off his father's debts and move out of the family home. In 1836 he married Catherine Hogarth, daughter of George Hogarth, the editor of the *Evening Chronicle*. In the same year he found fame and success with *Pickwick Papers*, first published in monthly instalments, later collected in a book.

Dickens' life changed rapidly from this point: the first of his ten children was born in 1837 and they moved to a larger house. He was upset by the sudden death of his sister-in-law, Mary Hogarth, when she was staying with them. He would later use her as inspiration for his young and beautiful female characters such as Rose Maylie in *Oliver Twist* (1838) and Little Nell in *The Old Curiosity Shop* (1841). These novels were both published in serial form like *Pickwick Papers* and became increasingly popular as people discussed what might happen next and waited for the next instalment. This public discussion of his work increased Dickens' fame.

In 1842, Dickens and his wife visited America and Canada, touring around and meeting his public. Although he was delighted by his celebrity and fame, he was annoyed that he did not receive any income from his American book sales as the United States had not signed any international copyright agreements. Although he was rich and famous, he still seemed to want more money and the security it perhaps represented. The trip had provided him with more material however, and he published his travel book, *American Notes for General Circulation*, later that year and *Martin Chuzzlewit* in serial form in 1843–4.

Back in England, Dickens continued to tour the country and became increasingly concerned about the inequality he saw around, especially in the cities. This concern helped to prompt him to write *A Christmas Carol*, a novella that followed the Victorian tradition of ghost stories but also carried a serious social and moral message. The story was another instant hit and was reprinted many times; it was still so popular many years later that he gave the first of many public readings in 1853 and read it in his farewell tour before his death in 1870.

It is thought Dickens based the characters of Fanny, Scrooge's sister, and Tiny Tim on his elder sister and her disabled son, Henry Jr. His sister Frances was known as Fanny and, although Dickens had been jealous of her when they were children because she was allowed to attend music college whilst he had to work, he realised this had not been her fault and their relationship became close and loving. In 1848 both Fanny and Henry Jr died; events that distressed Dickens greatly.

Fame and fortune continued for Dickens, and, in 1856, he purchased Gad's Hill Place, a large Georgian house in the country near Rochester. He had longed to live in this house since he had first seen it as a child and buying it was a symbol of all he had achieved. However, this did not mark a comfortable retirement – Dickens

DID YOU KNOW?

Dickens offended many of his American readers with his criticisms of their way of life.

CHECK THE NET

Dickens wrote a detailed letter to his friend, John Forster, describing his visit to his terminally ill sister. You can find it by going to **www.fidnet.com/ ~dap1955/dickens** and clicking on 'Family & Friends'.

could not stop working and he and his wife Catherine were struggling with their marriage.

It is now thought Catherine was suffering from post-natal depression, a form of depression felt by women after giving birth, but this was not understood at the time. Dickens' instant infatuation with an actress called Ellen Ternan, who was twenty-seven years younger than him, was the trigger that made him declare his marriage over. He had to be very careful to keep his relationship with Ellen out of the public eye as he knew that scandal would destroy his reputation. Catherine moved out of Gad's Hill and Dickens agreed to support her financially. They did not divorce, probably because of the scandal it would have caused. He and Ellen were very discreet, and often travelled overseas to be together.

Dickens continued to write and tour, ensuring his popularity remained high. However, his health began to deteriorate and doctors tried to warn him to slow down. The train crash at Staplehurst made Dickens wary of train travel but he could not avoid it if he wanted to continue his reading tours. He became very anxious before travelling and it is reported he would take brandy to help his nerves. Despite all this he continued to tour England, Ireland and America, ignoring his worsening health. In 1868, however, he admitted defeat and sailed home after cancelling planned readings in the USA and Canada. He decided to do one final tour, a 'Farewell Season', around England in 1869 but only managed seventy-four appearances before having to return home.

Dickens gave his last reading on 15 March 1870 and died suddenly at Gad's Hill on 9 June. He left behind one of the greatest literary mysteries of all in his unfinished novel, *The Mystery of Edwin Drood*, and in his other works one of the best collections of plots, characters and texts of any writer in his day or ours.

DID YOU KNOW?

As Dickens' health declined doctors allowed him to do twelve final readings as long as no rail travel was involved. This showed how much the train crash at Staplehurst still upset and affected him.

Now take a break!

CHARACTER MAP: *A CHRISTMAS CAROL*

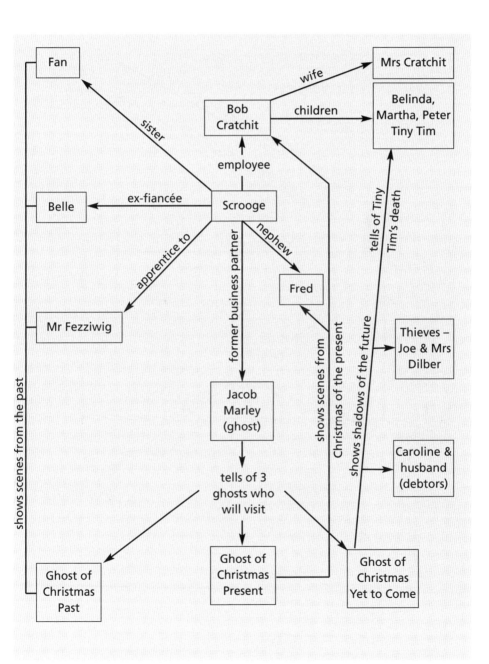

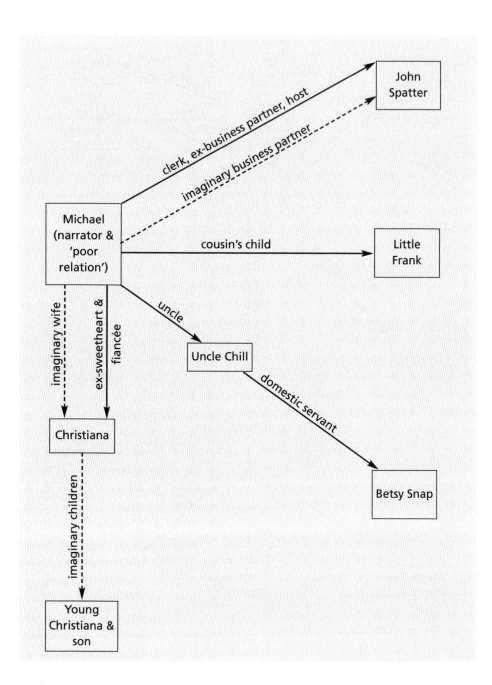

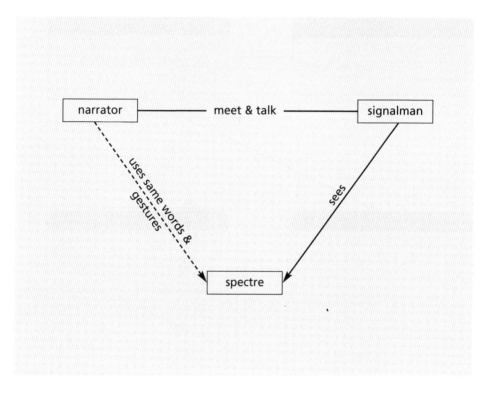

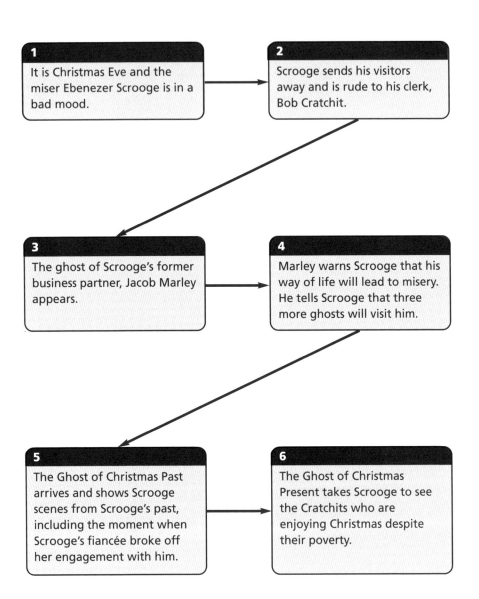

1 It is Christmas Eve and the miser Ebenezer Scrooge is in a bad mood.

2 Scrooge sends his visitors away and is rude to his clerk, Bob Cratchit.

3 The ghost of Scrooge's former business partner, Jacob Marley appears.

4 Marley warns Scrooge that his way of life will lead to misery. He tells Scrooge that three more ghosts will visit him.

5 The Ghost of Christmas Past arrives and shows Scrooge scenes from Scrooge's past, including the moment when Scrooge's fiancée broke off her engagement with him.

6 The Ghost of Christmas Present takes Scrooge to see the Cratchits who are enjoying Christmas despite their poverty.

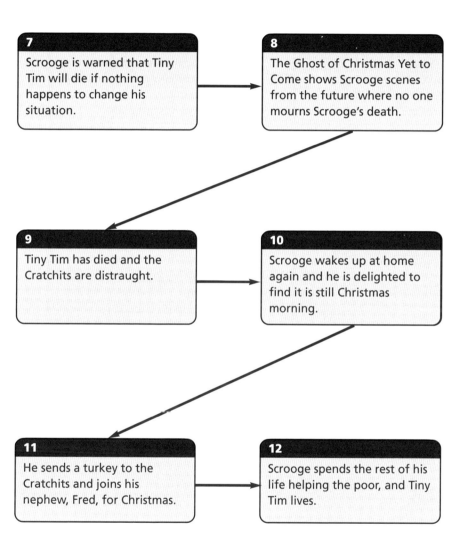

7

Scrooge is warned that Tiny Tim will die if nothing happens to change his situation.

8

The Ghost of Christmas Yet to Come shows Scrooge scenes from the future where no one mourns Scrooge's death.

9

Tiny Tim has died and the Cratchits are distraught.

10

Scrooge wakes up at home again and he is delighted to find it is still Christmas morning.

11

He sends a turkey to the Cratchits and joins his nephew, Fred, for Christmas.

12

Scrooge spends the rest of his life helping the poor, and Tiny Tim lives.

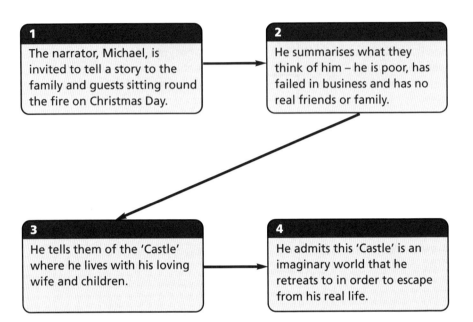

1
The narrator, Michael, is invited to tell a story to the family and guests sitting round the fire on Christmas Day.

2
He summarises what they think of him – he is poor, has failed in business and has no real friends or family.

3
He tells them of the 'Castle' where he lives with his loving wife and children.

4
He admits this 'Castle' is an imaginary world that he retreats to in order to escape from his real life.

TIMELINE: 'THE SIGNALMAN'

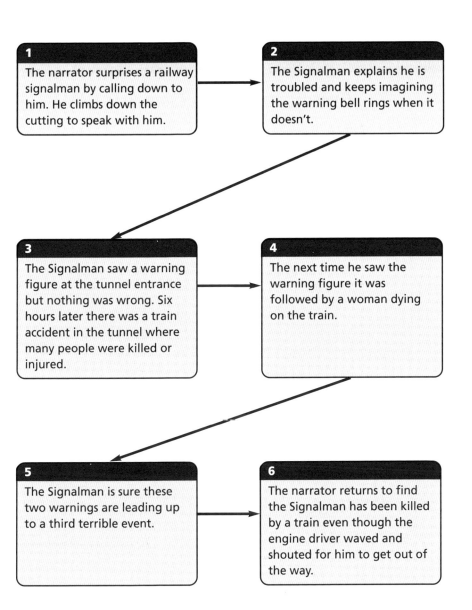

1
The narrator surprises a railway signalman by calling down to him. He climbs down the cutting to speak with him.

2
The Signalman explains he is troubled and keeps imagining the warning bell rings when it doesn't.

3
The Signalman saw a warning figure at the tunnel entrance but nothing was wrong. Six hours later there was a train accident in the tunnel where many people were killed or injured.

4
The next time he saw the warning figure it was followed by a woman dying on the train.

5
The Signalman is sure these two warnings are leading up to a third terrible event.

6
The narrator returns to find the Signalman has been killed by a train even though the engine driver waved and shouted for him to get out of the way.

Part Two

Summaries

General summary: *A Christmas Carol*

The Preface

Charles Dickens includes a note to his readers before the story begins. In it, he expresses his desire to raise a pleasant idea that will stay with the reader and not disturb them.

Stave One: Marley's Ghost

Jacob Marley, who was Ebenezer Scrooge's business partner, has been dead for seven years. Scrooge is so mean that rather than spend money painting out Marley's name above the door of the office he prefers to leave it as it is. Making money is the only thing he cares about.

The story focuses on one Christmas Eve. It is 3pm, cold and foggy. Scrooge is working hard and making sure his clerk, Bob Cratchit, is also working hard. Bob finds this difficult because he is so cold – Scrooge will only let him have one piece of coal for his fire.

Scrooge has four Christmas visitors: his nephew, Fred; two Charity Collectors; and a carol singer. Scrooge is rude to all of them and sends them away.

When Scrooge gets home something strange happens; he looks at his door knocker and sees the face of the dead Jacob Marley. He refuses to believe it but later Marley's ghost appears and tells Scrooge that his miserly way of life will lead to misery. Marley's Ghost warns Scrooge that three ghosts will visit him to show him the error of his ways.

Stave Two: The First of the Three Spirits

Scrooge wakes up in the dark and hears the church bell ringing. At 1am the Ghost of Christmas Past appears. He shows Scrooge the time when, as a little boy, he had to stay at school by himself over Christmas. He also shows Scrooge another time when his sister

---

CHECKPOINT 1

What impression do you gain of Scrooge from his behaviour in his office?

came to collect him. She had persuaded their father to let him return home and spend Christmas with them.

The Ghost then takes Scrooge to the house of Old Fezziwig, where Scrooge had his first job. They watch a jolly Christmas party and Scrooge notices how much happiness can be obtained from very little money.

Next, Scrooge sees himself as a young man. He is talking to Belle, his fiancée of that time. Belle breaks off the engagement because she thinks Scrooge loves money more than he loves her.

STAVE THREE: THE SECOND OF THE THREE SPIRITS

The next spirit to visit Scrooge is the Ghost of Christmas Present; he is a huge, jolly man, surrounded by Christmas food and decorations.

They visit the Cratchits' house and see the family preparing for their Christmas dinner with enthusiasm even though the goose they have to eat is very small. Bob Cratchit has been to church with Tiny Tim and tells the family how good and thoughtful Tiny Tim is.

Scrooge learns that Tiny Tim will not survive unless the future changes. This knowledge upsets Scrooge.

The Ghost takes Scrooge to see different groups of people enjoying themselves. Scrooge sees his nephew, Fred, with his family. They are discussing Scrooge and Fred is full of pity for him.

At the end of the night the Ghost shows Scrooge two children: a boy, called Ignorance, and a girl, called Want. The Ghost says they belong to Man and warns Scrooge to beware of them both, but especially to beware of Ignorance.

STAVE FOUR: THE LAST OF THE SPIRITS

The third ghost is the Ghost of Christmas Yet to Come; it is completely covered in black and very mysterious.

> **CHECKPOINT 2**
>
> Does Scrooge's unhappy childhood make you change your opinion of him?

> **CHECKPOINT 3**
>
> Why is the Ghost of Christmas Yet to Come shown to be so mysterious?

Scrooge is shown different conversations about a dead man. None of the people care that this man has died and the thieves have so little respect that they have stolen the clothes from his corpse.

In contrast, the Ghost then takes Scrooge to see the Cratchits who are deeply upset because Tiny Tim has died.

Finally, Scrooge is shown a gravestone with his own name on it. He realises he is the dead man the people were talking about. He at last promises to change his ways.

STAVE FIVE: THE END OF IT

Waking up in his own bed, Scrooge is delighted to be given a second chance and sets about making Christmas happy for everyone. He sends a turkey to the Cratchits, gives money to the Charity Collectors, and joins Fred for Christmas. The next day he raises Bob's wages and promises to become a friend to Tiny Tim, who does not die.

CHECK THE FILM

There are many excellent film versions of *A Christmas Carol*. Try the one directed by David Jones in 1999, starring Patrick Stewart and Richard E. Grant, and also *The Muppet Christmas Carol* (1993)!

Now take a break!

DETAILED SUMMARIES: *A CHRISTMAS CAROL*

THE PREFACE

A MESSAGE FROM CHARLES DICKENS

1 Dickens introduces the story and says that it has a specific idea behind it.

2 He hopes his readers won't be offended by this idea and will take it on board.

The short Preface is important because it tells us what Dickens is intending to do in the **novella**. He calls it a 'Ghostly little book' as it contains ghosts, and refers to his 'Ghost of an Idea' (Preface). This makes the idea sound insubstantial and rather harmless, and certainly not threatening. Dickens wants this idea to 'haunt' the 'house' of the reader – the house in this case is not just the reader's home, but also their body. He wants the reader to accept and embrace the ideas in this book, and not just dismiss them when they finish reading it. He uses the term 'lay' (Preface), which can mean to put away. When used in relation to ghosts, however, it means to exorcise a ghost, or stop one appearing.

STAVE ONE: MARLEY'S GHOST

[PP. 11–13] – EBENEZER SCROOGE

1 It is explained that Jacob Marley has been dead for seven years.

2 Ebenezer Scrooge, Marley's surviving business partner, is only interested in making money.

3 We are told that Scrooge is colder at heart than the winter weather.

The narrator goes to some lengths to assure us that Jacob Marley is dead, and has been for some time. The conversational tone helps us to trust this narrator. He addresses us directly, as though we were acquaintances of his, and we see no reason to question what we are

DID YOU KNOW?

Dickens wrote this story to be shared and read out loud at Christmas. He later toured, reading it to large audiences in Europe and America.

CHECKPOINT 4

Why does Dickens start by addressing the reader directly?

being told. The now **clichéd simile**, 'dead as a doornail' (Stave One, p. 11), is examined in a humorous, light-hearted way: it is pointed out that coffin nails must be 'deader' than doornails, if indeed, such objects have life in them anyway!

It is made clear that Scrooge knows that Marley is dead; indeed he was the only person directly affected by Marley's death. The repetition of 'sole' (Stave One, p. 11) emphasises the fact that Marley was so focused on business he didn't have time for any other friends or family. It also makes us think of the spiritual 'soul'; something this novella is concerned with.

Scrooge is described in very negative terms. The narrator provides a long list of adjectives, creating an overwhelming sense of Scrooge's character as cold, greedy and uncaring. The use of similes also adds to our impression of Scrooge, and this is before we have even met him. He is 'Hard and sharp as flint … solitary as an oyster' (Stave One, p. 12). Scrooge's physical appearance is described in equally unfavourable terms, all of which are linked to his miserly, ungenerous character – he has a 'pointed nose', 'shrivelled … cheeks' and a 'wiry chin' (Stave One, p. 12).

CHECK THE FILM

Patrick Stewart's portrayal of Scrooge in the film A *Christmas Carol* (1999) really emphasises his cold nature.

> ### The miserable Scrooge
> Here a clear link is established between Scrooge and bad weather. We are told the cold in his heart can be seen in his 'thin [blue] lips' and the 'frosty rime' on his head (Stave One, p. 12). The narrator jokes that the only difference between Scrooge and '[t]he heaviest rain, and snow, and hail, and sleet' (Stave One, p. 12) is that these unpleasant, wintry types of weather cover the world generously while Scrooge is always mean and miserly in his actions.

[PP. 13–20] – CHRISTMAS EVE AT THE OFFICE

❶ It is Christmas Eve and London is filled with fog.

❷ Scrooge's nephew comes to wish Scrooge a merry Christmas.

3 Two Charity Collectors ask Scrooge for money to help the poor.

4 Scrooge says Bob Cratchit may have Christmas Day off.

A traditional phrase, 'Once upon a time' (Stave One, p. 13) is used to signal the start of the story proper, and to establish this as a piece of fiction. It is a phrase many readers will know, and it gives the impression of a fairy tale.

The narrator introduces the image of Scrooge sitting counting money, even though it is Christmas Eve. It is cold, and the fog is almost alive, 'pouring in at every chink and keyhole' (Stave One, p. 13). This is an example of **pathetic fallacy**, where the weather reflects human emotions – in this case, Scrooge's bad temper is made visible in the fog. The fact it is getting everywhere demonstrates how infectious negative emotions can be.

Bob Cratchit, Scrooge's 'clerk' (Stave One, p. 13), is working in a smaller room, a 'cell' that Scrooge always watches. This suggests that Scrooge doesn't trust his clerk and also that Bob is a kind of prisoner there. Cratchit is really cold because Scrooge will only allow him one coal a day for his fire.

The atmosphere is transformed with the cheerful and jolly entrance of Scrooge's nephew, Fred. He has come to wish Scrooge a merry Christmas and represents all Scrooge is not. He is 'all in a glow' (Stave One, p. 14) because he has been walking fast, and is happy. This also suggests he has a warm personality, the opposite of Scrooge. Fred doesn't allow himself to be disheartened by Scrooge's gruff replies, and stands up for himself and his beliefs even though Scrooge calls him a fool. As well as providing a contrast to Scrooge in terms of character, we also learn that Fred does not have Scrooge's wealth – in fact, one of the reasons Scrooge calls Fred a fool is because he got married for love rather than money.

The argument about the value of Christmas continues, and it shows us how Scrooge thinks – he believes that financial profit is all that matters. Fred provides the opposite argument. His belief that men and women should 'open their shut-up hearts freely' (Stave One, p.

CHECKPOINT 5

What does Scrooge's treatment of Bob Cratchit tell us about these two characters?

GLOSSARY

rime a dull and dirty covering of frost

clerk a person employed in an office or bank to keep the records or accounts

DID YOU KNOW?

Bedlam was a hospital for people with mental health problems. These weren't really understood at the time and many people visited to see the patients as an amusement.

DID YOU KNOW?

Thomas Robert Malthus was an economist who used complicated economic calculations to predict that food supplies and resources would never be enough for the whole population, meaning that, for some, poverty and hunger were inevitable. Dickens did not agree with this.

CHECKPOINT 6

Are we meant to agree with Scrooge's or the Charity Collectors' view of charity and the poor?

15) and think of others as well as themselves is, in fact, the central argument of the whole **novella**.

As Fred leaves, he and Bob Cratchit wish each other a merry Christmas. Scrooge finds this incomprehensible as he does not understand how Cratchit can consider this a 'merry' time of year when he has to support his wife and children on only fifteen shillings a week. Scrooge feels he might as well 'retire to Bedlam' (Stave One, p. 16) as the whole world is going mad around him and he thinks it might be saner there.

Two 'portly gentlemen' (Stave One, p. 16) now enter and ask if they are speaking to Mr Scrooge or Mr Marley. This, and Scrooge's reply, reminds us yet again that Marley is dead. The gentlemen are Charity Collectors and want Scrooge to give them some money to help 'the poor and destitute, who suffer greatly at the present time' (Stave One, p. 17). Rather than give them money, Scrooge demands to know whether the prisons, the 'Union Workhouses' and the 'Treadmill and the Poor Law' (Stave One, p. 17) are still in operation. As far as he is concerned, these places are meant to provide for the poor and he doesn't see why he should contribute anything to them. He has to pay a tax to support these institutions, and he thinks that is enough. However, these places were well known for being hard and demeaning and the Charity Collectors point out that 'Many can't go there; and many would rather die' (Stave One, p. 17). This is when we really see Scrooge's harsh and callous nature: he thinks if the poor would rather die they should hurry up and do so as that would 'decrease the surplus population' (Stave One, p. 18). This is a disturbing idea to us, but Dickens is presenting an accepted economic theory of the time, suggested by Thomas Malthus. The Charity Collectors leave without any contribution from Scrooge.

As if in response to Scrooge's declaration, the 'fog and darkness thickened so' (Stave One, p. 18) and the narrator focuses on a church bell 'peeping slily down at Scrooge' (Stave One, p. 18). The **personification** of the bell makes it seem as if it is watching Scrooge. As it is a church bell, perhaps it is meant to represent the face of God watching over and judging Scrooge.

Away from Scrooge's office the atmosphere is very different; we are shown snapshots of people getting ready for the festive season – labourers gathered together enjoy a warming fire while traders display their goods with style. There are also carol singers on the street – but the singer who dares to stop outside Scrooge's door is chased rudely away by Scrooge.

Finally, the end of the working day arrives and Scrooge reluctantly admits this to Bob Cratchit who is keen to go home to his family and start his Christmas celebrations. Scrooge grudgingly agrees that Bob may have the whole of Christmas Day off – paid. He likens this to 'picking a man's pocket every twenty-fifth of December!' (Stave One, p. 19), because he feels he is being robbed by this custom. In recompense, Scrooge demands that Cratchit starts work early the following day.

We follow Bob Cratchit as he leaves, wrapped in his scarf or 'comforter' (Stave One, p. 19) as he does not own a winter coat. Despite this, he is full of the joys of the season – he goes down a slide twenty times and runs home to play blindman's-buff with his family.

Scrooge's journey home is quite different – he follows his usual routine, showing that he is not willing to make any changes for Christmas. He eats by himself at a tavern, reads the newspapers and does some work. Finally, he walks home. He lives in 'a gloomy suite of rooms' (Stave One, p. 20), stuck at the back of a dark and dreary yard. The fog is so thick now, that Scrooge has to find his way with his hands.

CHECKPOINT 7

Why does Dickens show us so many quick snapshots of people getting in the Christmas spirit?

GLOSSARY

Union Workhouses buildings where the homeless poor were given food and shelter. Conditions were very harsh; families were split up, food was poor quality and they had to work for up to ten hours a day

Treadmill a large metal wheel with steps on the outside so that a person walking up them would make the wheel move. This would be used to pump water or move grain. They were often used in prisons and sometimes found in workhouses as a punishment

Poor Law a law passed in 1834 that required harsh workhouses to be set up to take in the poor in every parish

CHECKPOINT 8

What does the different behaviour of Scrooge and Cratchit on their way home tell us about their characters?

Setting up the story

In this early part of the novella, Dickens not only describes the main character, Scrooge, in detail but also lays down the foundations for the story to come, and the moral message behind it. Scrooge is certainly not in the mood for celebrating Christmas – he sees it as a waste of time that could be better spent earning money. Fred and the Charity Collectors provide an alternative approach – one that looks out for others, especially those less fortunate. The stage is set for the action to take place, but the reader is also encouraged to think beyond it, to the social conditions of the world outside.

[PP. 20–30] – MARLEY APPEARS

❶ Scrooge's door knocker changes into the face of Marley.

❷ Marley's Ghost is covered with chains of keys, padlocks and other items associated with the money-lending business he and Scrooge ran together.

❸ Marley explains he is in torment because he only cared about money when he was alive and he now knows how wrong that was.

❹ Marley's Ghost tells Scrooge he will be visited by three spirits.

❹ Scrooge doesn't want to think about what has happened and goes straight to bed.

The narrator draws our attention to the door knocker, emphasising the fact there is nothing unusual about it except its large size. When it mysteriously changes into the face of Marley, Scrooge's dead business partner, the narrator again uses the **first person narrative** to ask if any reader can explain why the knocker has changed. We tend to forget it is the author who is making all this up when he makes a direct appeal to us in this way.

CHECKPOINT 9

Why does Dickens spend so much time describing the door knocker?

A whole paragraph is devoted to the description of this sight, helping the reader to visualise it, but also ensuring we understand its full significance – Scrooge isn't the sort of person who 'sees things' and Marley has been dead for years. This is the point at which Scrooge's Christmas becomes different for him.

The use of **similes** is rather unusual; the face has 'a dismal light about it, like a bad lobster in a dark cellar' (Stave One, p. 20). This suggests it has a strange, heavenly glow, indicating its otherworldliness.

As Scrooge looks at the face it becomes a knocker again, as if he had just imagined it. We are told he doesn't really react, but he does look behind the door before closing it, as if he expected to find the back of Marley's head sticking out. The narrator emphasises this by the repeated use of italics when we are told Scrooge '*did* pause' and '*did* look' (Stave One, p. 21). His expression of dismissal, 'Pooh, pooh!' (Stave One, p. 21), is perhaps an indication that the sight has affected him, and he feels the need to verbally reject it.

DID YOU KNOW?

In the Victorian era, before fridges were invented, shellfish and other perishables would have been kept in cold places such as cellars. If a lobster started to decay it would attract bacteria that glow in the dark (now known as photobacteria).

CHECKPOINT 10

Is Scrooge the hardened character he pretends to be?

The spooky atmosphere is built up further with the description of the sound of the door closing. The noise 'resounded through the house like thunder' reminding us of the poor weather outside. It is not just the echo of the door closing that can be heard, all the bottles of wine in the cellars below 'have a separate peal of echoes' (Stave One, p. 21). This reminds us of church bells ringing, a sound that will be heard throughout the novella signalling the arrival of each Ghost.

CHECKPOINT 11

Look at the description of Scrooge's journey upstairs (Stave One, p. 21). Why is it described so carefully and slowly?

Once upstairs, Scrooge checks all his rooms, indicating he has been unsettled by what he has seen. He closes his door and double locks himself in, something we are told 'was not his custom' (Stave One, p. 22), thus increasing our sense of unease. We are told of all the checks he makes; this list not only builds our knowledge of how Scrooge lives but also our sense of nervousness and suspense – we know something is going to happen.

Not only is Scrooge too mean to have a large fire at work, he is too mean to have a large one at home as well, and he has to sit near the fire to get any of its warmth. The fireplace surround has tiles with lots of pictures to illustrate stories from the Bible but when he looks at them all he can see is Marley's face. Scrooge refuses to believe it but has to walk across the room to get away from the sight, showing us that he is unnerved by what he has seen. When he sits down again he notices a bell that would have been used to communicate with other parts of the house before it was broken up into apartments. The bell, along with all the other bells in the house, rings out loudly for half a minute, a signal to Scrooge and to the reader that the events are about to begin.

Before we see the Ghost, Dickens uses sound to set up our expectations: there is 'a clanking noise deep down below' (Stave One, p. 22) and Scrooge remembers that ghosts drag chains. Dickens is careful to set this up before we see Marley to ensure we accept him as a ghost.

Marley's Ghost

Typically, Marley's Ghost is described for us in lots of detail so we are easily able to imagine what he looks like. The narrator emphasises the fact he looks the same as he always did, this means there can be no doubt that this is the ghost of Marley. What is different is that he is wrapped with chains made up with cash-boxes, keys, padlocks, books for recording business transactions and legal documents. All these are items relating to the money-lending business he ran with Scrooge, and are probably items used by Scrooge every day. These items represent or **symbolise** the aspects of life Marley focused on – he was more concerned with his business than other people.

Marley's Ghost sits down opposite Scrooge and asks why Scrooge doesn't believe what he is seeing and hearing, why he doubts his own senses. Scrooge suggests that this vision might just be a hallucination caused by indigestion and actually makes a joke, 'there's more of gravy than of grave about you' (Stave One, p. 24). He is suggesting that the Ghost has appeared as a result of him over-eating, rather than being a real visitor from the dead.

In order to make Scrooge listen, Marley's Ghost uses shock tactics: he unties the bandage (or folded handkerchief), which is holding his lower jaw up. As a result his jaw drops right down until it rests on his chest. This is a really horrifying image and is intended to stun Scrooge and the reader into listening to the Ghost. Until now the idea of a ghost has been mostly amusing, but this image of horror changes the tone and makes us realise the message we are going to hear is important.

Marley's Ghost now tells Scrooge of the terrible situation he is in. His punishment for being too concerned with making money when he was alive is to 'wander through the world – oh, woe is me! And witness what [I] cannot share but might have shared on earth, and turned to happiness!' (Stave One, p. 25). The language used to support these ideas is strong, words such as 'doomed', 'fettered' and 'ponderous' (Stave One, p. 25) add to the sense of weight and make us take this message seriously. As Scrooge is being told of his situation, so we are made to think of our own. The key here is that happiness comes from helping and working with other people, not from making as much money as possible.

Scrooge realises that his chain would be longer and heavier than that of Marley's Ghost, as he has spent seven more years than Marley behaving in the same way. He asks for comfort but Marley has none to give and adds that he cannot say all he would like to. This is a clever trick as it makes the reader use their own imagination to think of something worse than can be expressed in words, thus making the warning stronger, more personal, and more horrifying.

Marley's Ghost explains that Scrooge has a chance to escape the punishment or 'penance' (Stave One, p. 28) that he is suffering.

CHECKPOINT 12

Why do you think Scrooge makes a joke here?

 CHECK THE BOOK

In Shakespeare's play, *Hamlet*, the ghost of Hamlet's father appears to Hamlet and tells him that he was murdered by Hamlet's uncle. Because he died in his sleep without confessing his sins, he, like Marley's Ghost, is doomed to walk the earth, tortured by his conscience.

GLOSSARY

fettered restrained, held captive

ponderous heavy and tedious

penance penalty or punishment to wipe out a sin

CHECKPOINT 13

Why is the Ghost always referred to as 'it'?

DID YOU KNOW?

Dickens disagreed with the contents of the New Poor Law (see **Setting and background**), which was passed in 1834. It is probably this law he is blaming the government for here. He believed the law failed to help the poor in the way that society should.

CHECKPOINT 14

How do we know Scrooge has been affected by what has happened?

Three spirits will visit him, an idea Scrooge is not happy about, and show him how to avoid Marley's ghastly fate.

The Ghost opens the window and Scrooge sees the air full of similar, tormented ghosts. The language used to describe this scene emphasises its misery and horror, the sounds are 'incoherent' and 'inexpressibly sorrowful' (Stave One, p. 29). The ghosts are all suffering from being unable to help humans who are in need, something they didn't consider whilst they were alive but they now understand was key to their happiness and that of others. The scene is returned to reality and made political as the narrator suggests that ghosts of 'guilty governments' (Stave One, p. 30) are being made to suffer as a group for failing to help those in need.

The role of imagination

Here the narrator is using a similar technique to earlier, when we were made to imagine for ourselves the horrors Marley's Ghost is experiencing. By suggesting the wailing sounds the ghosts make are beyond the narrator's description, the reader has to use their imagination. Again, the scene is enhanced and enriched by the reader's own ideas of how terrible these ghosts might sound. It is an example of Dickens inviting his audience/readership to participate in the story.

Scrooge checks the door is still locked, which it is, and tries to dismiss the events with his usual expression of disgust and rejection, 'Humbug!' (Stave One, p. 30), but fails to get past the first syllable. This suggests to the reader that even though he tries to behave as usual, and tries to reject all that has happened, he is not able to and part of him is deeply affected by what has passed.

Stave Two: The First of the Three Spirits

[pp. 31–3] – Waiting for the First Visitor

❶ The clock bell rings twelve times even though Scrooge went to bed after 2am.

❷ The first Ghost arrives just after 1am.

As Scrooge awakes it is so dark he can't see the difference between the wall and the window, even though the window is transparent. He listens for the clock bell of a nearby church to tell him the time. Once again a reference is made to a church bell, linking to the idea of God watching over Scrooge, making judgements about him.

Scrooge is astonished when the bell rings twelve times, to show it is midnight. Part of the reason for his confusion is he knows he went to bed after midnight and he can't believe he has slept through a whole day and into the next night. He checks his own watch, his 'repeater' but it also rings twelve times.

He tries to look out the window but first has to rub the frost off with his sleeve, reminding us that it is really cold weather. It is also very foggy, perhaps a **metaphor** for Scrooge's cloudy and blinkered view of the world. He can't see or hear anyone so decides it's still the night-time and returns to bed to try to sleep.

Scrooge remembers Marley's Ghost told him the first visitor would arrive shortly after 1am and decides he will stay awake to ensure there is no chance of dreaming about ghosts; then he realises he couldn't sleep even if he wanted to. This lets us know how tense and worried he is about what might happen – a state of mind that is very much out of character for the hardened Scrooge.

As the bell rings for 1am Scrooge is triumphant as he thinks all is well and he is safe from any visitor. However, as the hour bell sounds, lights flash in his room and the curtains that hang around his bed frame are drawn open. The narrator emphasises the close proximity of this Ghost and draws the reader into the story by telling the reader that the Ghost was as close to Scrooge as the narrator is to him. This reminds us this story was written to be read out loud to groups at Christmas and makes us feel physically close to what is happening.

CHECKPOINT 15

Why does Dickens describe the wait in so much detail?

GLOSSARY

incoherent something unclear and which cannot be understood

repeater a clock which chimes or makes a sound on the hour, and every quarter. It can be made to chime the time on demand

DID YOU KNOW?

Dickens loved acting. He took part in lots of amateur performances, even one which was performed in front of Queen Victoria. It is clear how much Dickens was influenced by the theatre in his writing. You can see this in his direct relationship with his readers and the way he builds drama and tension.

Increasing the tension

We know a ghost is about to visit but Dickens makes this more dramatic by building up atmosphere and suspense. The reminders of the cold, dark weather outside and chimings of the clock's bell contribute to the sinister atmosphere. Counting the time builds suspense further and makes us uneasy. As 1am approaches, we, like Scrooge, wonder what will happen.

[PP. 33–4] – THE GHOST OF CHRISTMAS PAST

❶ The Ghost looks like a child and like an old man at the same time.

❷ It is the Ghost of Scrooge's past.

The description of the Ghost is detailed and apparently contradictory; it is like a child and like an old man all at the same time. It has long white hair but its face is unwrinkled and its skin has a youthful glow to it. It is strong and muscular but also delicate. These apparent contradictions can be explained when we realise this is the Ghost of Scrooge's past, and it therefore has the physical properties of his youth – hence the 'tenderest bloom' (Stave Two, p. 33) on its skin. However, Scrooge is now an old man and it is a long time since he was a child. The physical properties of the Ghost thus resemble the memories of childhood – the memories are old and perhaps dulled, but they are nevertheless made up of youthful moments. The Ghost's clothing continues this theme; it holds a branch of holly, **symbolising** winter, but its robe is trimmed with summer flowers.

CHECKPOINT 16

What impression have you gained of this Ghost?

Although it is dark Scrooge is able to see everything clearly because 'a bright jet of clear light' (Stave Two, p. 33) is shining up from the Ghost's head. The Ghost itself is also a source of light, and parts of its body glow for a moment and then fade, becoming invisible. This elaborate and fantastical description creates a clear image for the reader to visualise and makes the Ghost somehow seem more real: its unusual appearance is certainly more than Scrooge would be able to invent.

The Ghost's voice is 'soft and gentle' (Stave Two, p. 34) and appears to come from a distance away; perhaps this is intended to add to the impression that the Ghost has come from the past.

The power of light

Scrooge can't bear the light that is emitting from the Ghost's head and asks him to put his hat back on, which he does. This shows us that Scrooge is uncomfortable in the presence of this being, especially with the pure light that it emits. Light is traditionally associated with purity and truth, traits often linked to childhood. So here, Scrooge's reaction to the light coming from the Ghost might indicate that he recognises the difference between the purity of his childhood, and the life he is now living. Dickens will later use the sunny light of Christmas morning to symbolise new hope for Scrooge.

Scrooge tries to recover his old security and demands to know why the Ghost is there. He might not be comfortable with what is happening but he still tries to gain the upper hand. The Ghost's answer, that he is there for Scrooge's welfare, doesn't convince Scrooge who thinks that a good night's sleep would be much more useful. As if the Ghost can read Scrooge's mind he changes the answer to 'Your reclamation' (Stave Two, p. 34), which is much stronger and reminds us of the selfish path Scrooge has followed.

The Ghost takes Scrooge by the hand and to the window. Scrooge is frightened but there is no point in him struggling against it: the grip is gentle but 'not to be resisted' (Stave Two, p. 34). This reminds us of the power of memory, and perhaps of fate too.

[PP. 35–40] – SCROOGE'S CHILDHOOD

1. The Ghost of Christmas Past shows Scrooge how, as a boy, he had to spend Christmas at school.

2. His sister, Fan, arrives to take him home after persuading their father to let him return to the family.

3. The old Scrooge responds emotionally to these memories.

 CHECK THE NET
You can find the original illustrations that accompanied the 1843 first edition of *A Christmas Carol* on the University of Glasgow's website. Go to **http://special.lib.gla.ac.uk** and find the Book of the Month for December 1999.

GLOSSARY

reclamation to reclaim or get something back, in this case Scrooge's soul

CHECKPOINT 17

What exactly does the contrast between the countryside and the city suggest?

The Ghost takes Scrooge to the countryside where he grew up. Its fields and clean air are a real contrast to the city. Dickens presents this as an idyllic scene, away from the dirt and pollution of London where grief and greed are found everywhere.

A change in Scrooge?

Scrooge's response to being shown the countryside of his childhood is immediate: his lip trembles, there is a catch in his voice, and the Ghost suggests he is crying. This is very different behaviour to that we have seen so far in Scrooge and it is interesting that he can change so quickly. Perhaps it is being caught off-guard that has caused this reaction. Scrooge's show of emotion means we have to start re-assessing our response to him. At the same time, however, it's important we don't forget all that we have previously learnt about this character.

Once again **personification** and **pathetic fallacy** are used to create the atmosphere and emphasise the contrast between the countryside and the city. Boys are laughing and having fun and their shouts and laughter echo around the fields. The narrator goes as far as saying 'the crisp air laughed to hear it' (Stave Two, p. 35), suggesting that the air is so full of the sound of laughter it is as if the air is laughing itself. This conveys a joyful, happy atmosphere far from the oppressive, dismal atmosphere of the city.

The boys are running home from the school they stay in during the term time. One child has not gone home for Christmas, and, as Scrooge reacts emotionally to this scene it becomes clear that he was the boy who had to stay at school for Christmas. The narrator allows us to work this out for ourselves. This makes us more involved in the story and increases our sympathy for Scrooge. The short statements that confirm this, 'Scrooge said he knew it. And he sobbed' (Stave Two, p. 36) are bleak and moving. The lack of detail suggests that Scrooge is too upset to develop the description. His emotional state is a total contrast to that of the proud, mean-spirited man we met in Stave One.

CHECKPOINT 18

What is your response to Scrooge at this point?

The lonely young boy does have some comfort; we see the wonderful characters from the book he is reading – Ali Baba, the Genii and Robinson Crusoe's parrot are among the fantastical figures that appear. This scene emphasises the power of the imagination and shows the comfort fiction can bring. Scrooge is animated as he comments on all the characters. Reminded of his own childhood, he now regrets his treatment of the young carol singer whom he chased away (Stave One, p. 19).

The Ghost takes Scrooge to see another Christmas, in the same room but time must have passed as it is shabbier and dirtier. Scrooge's younger sister, Fan, darts in, changing the atmosphere – she is full of life and joy and has come to collect young Scrooge so he can join the family for Christmas. This is a touching scene, made sharper by the recognition that the only reason the young Scrooge was left at school by himself over Christmas was that his father didn't want him at home.

Fan tells the young Scrooge of their father's change in character and describes their home as 'heaven' (Stave Two, p. 38). The idea that their father has been able to transform himself from someone who sends his son away and refuses to have him in the house, to a parent who makes a home heavenly, suggests that Scrooge too can change.

To top it all, the young Scrooge will not have to return to the school but is 'to be a man' (Stave Two, p. 38), suggesting that he will be apprenticed and start to learn a trade.

DID YOU KNOW?

Dickens was devoted to his own sister, also called Fanny, and was devastated when she died.

Before he leaves the school, the young Scrooge and his sister have a glass of poor quality wine and some indigestible cake with the schoolmaster. This little scene is typical of Dickens – it is humorous and telling. Everything seems to be done for show – the 'best parlour' is freezing cold and even the traditional pictures and fittings have been affected by the cold. They are offered a glass of 'curiously light wine' and a piece of 'curiously heavy cake' (Stave Two, p. 39). Dickens' description is amusing because cake is supposed to be light and wine is meant to have 'body' or depth to it. The use of the adverb 'curiously' implies the viewpoint of the narrator, and reminds us that it is he who is relaying the events. Use of vocabulary such as this is typical of Dickens' work.

After the children have departed the school the Ghost speaks of Scrooge's sister and we see real enthusiasm and love for her from Scrooge. When the Ghost reminds Scrooge that his sister, although now dead, had a son Scrooge becomes uneasy. We realise that this son must be his nephew Fred and that Scrooge is now regretting his behaviour to Fred in the same way as he regretted his treatment of the carol singer.

Scrooge's childhood

We are shown that Scrooge had an unhappy childhood, but knew love from his sister. This relationship was obviously very important to him. It seems that Scrooge experienced sad, lonely times in his childhood but also happy ones too. Reconnecting with these past feelings – either of being lonely and vulnerable, or of being joyful and surrounded by loved ones – enables him to begin to feel sympathy with others. Tiny Tim is another example of how Dickens uses the symbol of a child to encourage good feelings in other people.

[PP. 40–3] – FEZZIWIG'S PARTY

1 We learn that Scrooge was apprenticed to a man called Fezziwig.

2 Fezziwig and his whole family throw a Christmas party.

3 Everyone has a wonderful time but the Ghost asks why the people are so grateful to Fezziwig when the party cost little money.

4 Scrooge defends Fezziwig and explains how much happiness he has given.

The contrast with Christmas at Fezziwig's and the Christmas we saw at Scrooge's office is vast; everyone is working hard but at seven o'clock Fezziwig declares everyone must stop work so they may have their Christmas party. Fezziwig is an attractive character: his voice is 'comfortable, oily, rich, fat, jovial' (Stave Two, p. 40) which gives a sense of plenty, even over-indulgence. This could be off-putting, but the verbs used to describe his movements combine to make him lively and warm. He 'laughed all over himself', and skips with 'wonderful agility' (Stave Two, p. 40).

The family join the party and are described in similar terms. Mrs Fezziwig is 'one substantial smile' and the three daughters are 'beaming and loveable' (Stave Two, p. 41). All who work for the Fezziwigs have been invited to this party. The inclusion of the 'boy from over the way' and the 'girl from next door but one' (Stave Two, p. 41) whose employers are not as generous as the Fezziwigs shows that not everyone behaves in the same way he does. The only explanation for Fezziwig throwing such a party is that he is a kind and generous person who cares about others.

As the party ends Mr and Mrs Fezziwig say goodbye to each person as they leave, showing they are not too important to speak to the different employees who attended. The two apprentices, Scrooge and Dick, sleep in the back-shop, reminding us of the working conditions of the time. Fezziwig is not a rich employer and has to

CHECKPOINT 19

Fezziwig provides a direct contrast with Scrooge. Why has Dickens done this?

run his business every day. But he has thrown the party out of choice, to show how much he appreciates his employees.

Scrooge has enjoyed every moment of the party, to the extent that he temporarily forgets the Ghost. Perhaps to provoke Scrooge, the Ghost dismisses what Fezziwig achieved as 'A small matter … to make these silly folks so full of gratitude' (Stave Two, p. 43). As the Ghost points out, Fezziwig didn't spend much money on the party, but the two apprentices spend the night praising him. Scrooge leaps to Fezziwig's defence explaining that happiness doesn't have a monetary value, it is the fact Fezziwig chooses to throw such a party and spend his time with his workers that makes the difference. The value of personal contributions over financial aid is emphasised here. The reader is guided to think of Scrooge's own behaviour to Bob Cratchit as Scrooge regrets his earlier actions.

CHECK THE FILM

The film, *Scrooged*, starring Bill Murray came out in 1984. It is a modernisation of the story of *A Christmas Carol* where a selfish television executive is haunted by three spirits on Christmas Eve. It shows how Dickens' message can easily be adapted to a modern day setting.

[PP. 43–8] – THE BROKEN ENGAGEMENT

❶ The Ghost shows Scrooge himself as a young man with his fiancée, Belle.

❷ Scrooge's face already reveals his love of money.

❸ Belle breaks their engagement because she says Scrooge loves money more than he loves her.

❹ Belle marries someone else and has a loving family and a happy life.

The final memory Scrooge is taken to see is a meeting between him as a young man and Belle, the young woman he was once engaged to marry. We are given a clear description of his appearance to highlight his cares and concerns. Although he is still a young man, 'There was an eager, greedy, restless motion in the eye, which showed the passion that had taken root' (Stave Two, p. 43). This 'passion' is the love of money, also called avarice, which is responsible for turning Scrooge into the miserly old man we first met.

Belle breaks off their engagement, saying Scrooge now loves money more than he loves her. She calls money his 'idol' (Stave Two, p. 44), suggesting that he not only loves it but also worships it as a false god. This Scrooge is far removed from the young boy who was apprenticed to Fezziwig and had so much energy at the party. We read their discussion with interest to find out what has made him change so much.

We learn that Scrooge has ambition to prosper and achieve success in the world, and that he once wanted to succeed for them both but now, as Belle says, the 'nobler aspirations' have gone, leaving only 'the master passion, Gain' (Stave Two, p. 44). He is no longer the man she fell in love with, and furthermore, Belle knows she is now not the sort of woman Scrooge values because she is still poor. She leaves him wishing him happiness 'in the life you have chosen' (Stave Two, p. 45).

Free will

Dickens shows here how events from our past shape us and our understanding of the world. However, he implies that we still have free will enough to choose our own paths. Scrooge clearly had a choice at this point to have a happy life shared with Belle, or devote himself to the selfish pursuit of wealth. Dickens shows how society also played a part in Scrooge's obsession. Scrooge's empoverished early childhood and rejection by his father could be seen as reasons why he wants to acquire his own wealth and security. Although these factors may have contributed to his miserliness, Scrooge still had the opportunity to change his mind.

This scene obviously affects Scrooge badly as he calls it 'torture' (Stave Two, p. 46). The Ghost still has one final scene to show him. We see an older Belle, with a daughter the age Belle was in the previous scene, at home and happy. Belle has a loving family and husband and the room is full of laughter and energy. This scene is not one from Scrooge's memory, but is presented to show him what he could have had if he had chosen Belle instead of money. To make matters worse, Belle's husband tells her he saw Scrooge sitting in his office by himself 'quite alone in the world' (Stave Two, p. 47). The

 CHECK THE BOOK

Have a look at how Michael's courtship with Christiana is handled in 'The Poor Relation's Story'. Are there similarities between Scrooge and Uncle Chill, and how does the scene showing Belle happily married compare to Michael's perfect vision of life with Christiana in the 'Castle'?

GLOSSARY

idol a false god, or an image of a god used as a focus for worship

contrast is effective and the point clear – love of money can destroy human love.

Scrooge cannot bear this final scene and begs to be taken from it. He struggles with the Ghost, much as one might struggle with bad memories. Eventually, Scrooge seizes the Ghost's hat and pulls it down so the light coming from its head can no longer be seen. With this the Ghost disappears and Scrooge falls asleep once more.

CHECKPOINT 20
Why does Scrooge pull down the Ghost's hat?

STAVE THREE: THE SECOND OF THE THREE SPIRITS

[PP. 49–52] – THE GHOST OF CHRISTMAS PRESENT

❶ Scrooge wakes before 1am and fearfully waits for the next Ghost.

❷ The Ghost of Christmas Present appears in the next room.

❸ He is surrounded with Christmas food and holding a torch of fire.

Scrooge wakes up suddenly, and knows another ghost is about to appear. When he thinks about what is about to happen he opens all the curtains around his bed so that he will see the ghost appear rather then allowing it to surprise him. This behaviour is consistent with Scrooge's earlier actions. He still wants to be in control of everything that happens. This is our first indication that the visit from the Ghost of Christmas Past hasn't changed Scrooge very much.

CHECKPOINT 21
What do you think? Has Scrooge changed or is he just trying to say the right things to get through the visits as quickly as possible?

Scrooge's struggle

We see Scrooge's true feelings when the bell strikes one and he is 'taken with a violent fit of trembling' (Stave Three, p. 50). This reaction shows Scrooge's fear, but it is important to see that he is fighting the suggestions the Ghosts have made. The final change in Scrooge has to be a real and permanent one. At this stage he has not yet seen enough for a permanant transformation to take place.

Scrooge sees a light coming from the next room. He enters to be faced with a transformed room and the next Ghost. The room is decorated with greenery from plants such as holly and mistletoe and there is a great fire in the fireplace, bigger than any fire the miserly Scrooge had ever made. The descriptions of plenty are similar to those elsewhere in the text – here, the list of foodstuffs is overwhelming. All this food is piled high to make a throne for the giant Ghost who carries a torch of fire.

Scrooge's determination not to be afraid or surprised has gone. He enters 'timidly' and looks at the Ghost 'reverently' (Stave Three, p. 51). These adverbs make us sorry for Scrooge and show that he does have the ability to be humble. The Ghost speaks kindly and asks if Scrooge has ever seen any of his fellow ghosts or brothers, of which there are more than eighteen hundred. The mean, uncharitable side of Scrooge responds by considering how much it must cost to provide for so many people. However, Scrooge has learnt from his first experience that he will be taken on a journey and so 'submissively' (Stave Three, p. 52) asks the Ghost to do as he will.

DID YOU KNOW?

'More than eighteen hundred' (Stave Three, p. 51) is the number of Christmases there have been since the first Christmas of Jesus' birth when our calendar began. This reminds us that this novella was written in 1843 and set around that time.

[PP. 52–6] CHRISTMAS IN THE CITY

1. The weather is bad, but people are full of joy.
2. There is a sense of excess and celebration in the City.
3. People who can't afford their own ovens take their Christmas meals to be cooked at the bakers.
4. The Ghost sprinkles incense on meals and people.
5. Scrooge questions the reason for closing everything on Sundays.

Scrooge is taken to the City where the weather is still severe, with snow everywhere. However, the people out in the snow get on with clearing it and the narrator likens the sound of the work to music. Perhaps this suggests that such work, when many people are sharing it, can be joyful. In contrast with this impression, the houses and their windows are black, as a result of the soot from chimneys and

www. **CHECK THE NET**

Smog was a real problem in Dickens' London. Smog is caused by factories belching out smoke which mixes with fog in the air to form a thick, polluted atmosphere. For more information go to **www.met-office.gov.uk** and search for 'smog'.

factories which covered London. The pure and 'smooth white sheet of snow upon the roofs' (Stave Three, p. 52) is also contrasted with the soot and the dirty snow on the roads where carts and wagons have ploughed it up, much as our cars turn white snow to dirty slush today. The narrator goes on to highlight the problems of soot and smog that 'choked up' streets (Stave Three, p. 52), even in the summer. This was a key concern at the time of writing, and when we think back to the country scene of Scrooge's childhood we understand Dickens' concern.

The people who are out clearing the snow are full of energy and joy, throwing the occasional snowball and laughing with each other. The narrator creates a real sense of a community working together. There are detailed descriptions of the shops still open and full of Christmas foods and goods – once again the long lists of adjectives create a sense of abundance. The goods might be different, but the description of shops piled high, offering so many opportunities for purchasing and consumption isn't much removed from Christmas today.

When the church bell rings, the 'good people' are called to church (Stave Three, p. 55). We soon realise, however, that the term 'good' may only be applied to those who have the means to go to church, i.e., those who have enough money to employ servants to tend their houses and do the cooking. Those without the ability to cook their Christmas dinners at home take them to the bakers to put them in the oven. Those people who go to church are not necessarily better than those who don't, rather, it is implied, they are just more privileged in terms of time and living conditions.

The Ghost doesn't go to the church, instead he stands in the baker's doorway and sprinkles incense from his torch on their dinners and even on them when they are angry. He suggests that the poor need support and intervention more than those who are in the church. This comment makes Scrooge question the call to stop all work on Sundays, for this would 'cramp these people's opportunities of innocent enjoyment' by depriving 'them of their means of dining every seventh day' (Stave Three, p. 56).

A Christmas Carol, Stave Three

Poverty in London

Scrooge is voicing an argument often forwarded by Dickens against Sabbatarianism. However, it should be remembered that the people Scrooge is calling poor do have food and shelter – there was a further level of poverty where people were destitute. The contrast between the pure white snow and the soot can be seen to reflect the difference in living conditions between the rich and the poor in the City. In Victorian London very poor families often lived only a short distance from much more wealthy people and so the contrasts were particularly acute.

[PP. 56–64] – CHRISTMAS AT THE CRATCHITS'

1 It is Christmas Day and Mrs Cratchit and some of the Cratchit children are preparing for their Christmas meal with excitement.

2 Bob returns from church with Tiny Tim on his shoulder.

3 The family enjoy their meal even though it isn't really enough for them.

5 Scrooge is told Tiny Tim will die if the future doesn't change.

The Ghost takes Scrooge to the Cratchits where they have all made an effort to make Christmas special. The 'four-roomed house' (Stave Three, p. 56) is based on the house Dickens lived in as a child. Mrs Cratchit's gown has been mended and patched up many times but she has added ribbons, which are cheap, to make it seem better. She and her daughter are described as being 'brave' (Stave Three, p. 57) in these ribbons, showing us they know they are not well dressed, but are making the most of their situation.

The family is described with a sense of positive energy; they are all taking part in the preparations for Christmas, and 'two smaller Cratchits' come 'tearing in, screaming' (Stave Three, p. 57) about how wonderful their goose smells as it cooks. Like many of the poorer families they have an open fire, but no oven, so they have taken their goose to be cooked at the bakers. The narrator gently mocks their enthusiasm; they have no way of distinguishing the

DID YOU KNOW?

Dickens disagreed with the Sabbatarian Movement which argued for a strict observance of Sunday as a day of rest and worship. Dickens argued this limited the rights of the lower classes as they had to work all week, including Saturday, and only had Sunday to enjoy recreational activities higher classes were able to enjoy all week.

CHECKPOINT 22

How does this scene contrast with Scrooge's lifestyle?

smell of their goose from all the others cooking alongside it. However, our impression of them is favourable due to the overwhelming sense of energy and enthusiasm included in the scene; the children 'danced about the table' and even the potatoes are described as knocking on the lid of the saucepan 'to be let out and peeled' (Stave Three, p. 57).

The sense of fun in the family is extended as they hear their father, Bob Cratchit, returning from church with Tiny Tim. Martha, one of their daughters, hides and Mrs Cratchit joins in with the joke, pretending to Bob that Martha is not able to join them. This incident gives us a real sense of the close family unit that Dickens is promoting, and that Scrooge is lacking. There is laughter and joy, and, despite their social position and financial situation, there is happiness.

CHECK THE BOOK

The New Testament of the Bible relates over thirty miracles Christians believe were performed by Jesus, mainly by curing the sick and disabled. Have a look at the Gospels of Mark or Luke for examples.

Tiny Tim, perhaps one of Dickens' most famous characters, is introduced as a figure deserving of sympathy – the narrator comments on his inability to walk unaided, before describing his personality. Tim has been to church with his father and 'hoped the people saw him in the church, because he was a cripple, and it might be pleasant to them to remember upon Christmas Day who made lame beggars walk and blind men see' (Stave Three, p. 58). Tim's hope that the sight of his disability will remind the other church-goers of Jesus Christ, whose birthday they are, after all, celebrating, is presented as evidence of his purity and innocence. He is offered as a role model for children and adults, and may be read as a **metaphor** for the condition of the poor in society. Tim is not able to survive without external support. However, the support that is available to him is the 'iron frame' and 'little crutch' (Stave Three, p. 57) which, Dickens suggests, entrap as much as they support. This is a metaphor for the fact that the poor in Victorian England could only survive day-to-day by working in poorly-paid positions such as Bob Cratchit's, which allowed them to maintain their standard of living, but never improve it.

Tiny Tim

The physically disabled saintly child is a stock character from Victorian literature and causes problems for readers today due to the **sentimental** excess with which he is presented. Essentially, Dickens uses Tim to provoke sympathy and elicit support for his social message. However difficult a modern reader might find this use of a disabled character, it must be remembered that Victorian England was a very different place, where such characters had no independent means. The economy valued those who were able to contribute physically, especially with the move from agricultural to industrial manufacture. Dickens finds a 'use' for such people – to encourage charitable giving and support his moral message. With Tiny Tim he was very successful.

Even though the family treat their Christmas meal as a feast it is clear to us that it isn't really enough for them. It is 'eked out' (Stave Three, p. 60), meaning made to go further, by the stuffing, potatoes and apple sauce, all much cheaper ingredients. When the tiny pudding is also brought out, the fact that all the family praise it and none of them will acknowledge how small it is shows the Crachits' sense of pride that they are surviving and achieving despite their social situation.

DID YOU KNOW?
According to Peter Ackroyd's biography of Dickens it is estimated that in 1839 almost half of all funerals in London were for children younger than ten years old.

The reality of Tiny Tim's poor health undermines all this enjoyment, however. The clear message is that conditions must change if he is to survive, and the Ghost uses Scrooge's earlier harsh words to shame Scrooge into realising the role he has played in the Crachits' poverty. The Ghost questions the power that some people have assumed to 'decide what men shall live, what men shall die' (Stave Three, p. 63). This strong speech affects Scrooge greatly, and is also a comment on the Malthusian theories Dickens so strongly opposed (see **Setting and background**).

Finally, the Cratchits sit around the fire and Bob proposes a toast to Scrooge, as 'Founder of the Feast' (Stave Three, p. 63) – after all it is the money Scrooge pays Bob as wages that has paid for their meal. Mrs Cratchit is not nearly as charitable as Bob and has to be reminded not to say what she thinks of her husband's employer because the children are present. Her function is to ensure the reader knows the **irony** of toasting Scrooge when the Cratchits have been so overwhelmed by such a small feast.

[PP. 65–6] – Christmas around the country

❶ The Ghost shows Scrooge a family of miners celebrating Christmas with good cheer.

❷ Two lighthouse keepers, who are isolated, share some of the spirit of the season.

❸ A ship, far from the shore, contains men who are full of Christmas thoughts.

The Ghost takes Scrooge to see three further scenes, all of which contain people full of hope at Christmas. The miner's family are a 'cheerful company' (Stave Three, p. 65); the whole family have assembled in their best clothes and join the oldest of them in singing a song. Beyond the shoreline, on 'a dismal reef of sunken rocks' (Stave Three, p. 66), two lighthouse keepers turn their standard meal into a Christmas dinner and wish each other the best for the season. Finally, far out at sea, on a ship, sailors gain hope from the idea of Christmas and all 'had a kinder word for one another on that day than on any other day in the year' (Stave Three, p. 66).

Creating a sense of community

These three scenes act as a series of tableaux, or pictures, and capture the essence of what Dickens thinks Christmas should be about. None of the people have the material possessions that Scrooge could afford, but all gain some comfort from a sense of shared humanity and companionship. These scenes also reinforce the message of the Crachit family. Dickens reminds us that Christmas is above all about valuing people rather than anything that money can buy.

 CHECK THE NET

The Victoria & Albert Museum holds a copy of the first ever Christmas card. You can see it online by going the homepage **www.vam.ac.uk** and typing 'christmas card' into the search engine.

[PP. 67–72] – CHRISTMAS AT FRED'S

1 Scrooge's nephew, Fred, and his family are having fun at Christmas.

2 They discuss Scrooge, and decide the only person he harms by being so mean is himself.

3 Scrooge joins in with the games they play although they cannot see or hear him.

Fred, Scrooge's nephew, behaves as he did when we first met him in Scrooge's office; he is cheerful and merry and refuses to be negative about anything or anyone. The scene is full of laughter, and is very attractive because of its **juxtaposition** with the preceding Christmas celebrations we have seen. Fred recounts his meeting with Scrooge but decides 'his offences carry their own punishment' (Stave Three, p. 68), providing us with another reason for charity and compassion. This scene acts as a counter or balance to Christmas with the Cratchits; there we were shown why we should help others, now we are shown how generosity will also benefit the giver.

This scene is saved from being one that merely preaches a message by the characterisation and humour it contains. Fred and his wife are clearly in tune with each other, and the amorous pursuit of Fred's sister-in-law by Topper is humorous and lightens the atmosphere.

CHECK THE BOOK

The idea of an innocent child had been explored by William Blake in his poems *Songs of Innocence and of Experience* (1789). Although many critics have commented on the similarity in perspective in Dickens' work, he did not have any work by Blake in his extensive library.

A musical tune that Scrooge remembers his sister playing or singing softens Scrooge, and he forgets himself and his normal demeanour as he watches the children playing party games. This section of the novella reminds us that fun can be had without hurting anyone and without spending much money. As the narrator tells us, 'it is good to be children sometimes' (Stave Three, p. 69). Here Dickens reinforces the concept of the child as innocent, a key idea in literature of this time.

In a parallel to the Cratchits' Christmas celebrations, the group drink a toast to Scrooge, this time reasoning that he has given them cause for laughter. Fred reminds us that Scrooge wouldn't accept his Christmas wishes earlier, but he gives them anyway, showing that such thoughts don't cost anything. By this point Scrooge is attempting to actively participate in the scene. He is unable to however, and the Ghost takes Scrooge away again, showing him many other different Christmas scenes where the Ghost leaves his blessings.

[PP. 72–3] – IGNORANCE AND WANT

❶ The Ghost shows Scrooge two children called Ignorance and Want.

❷ They are the children of the society in which Scrooge lives.

❸ The Ghost says both are bad, but Ignorance is more dangerous than Want.

CHECK THE NET

You can find stills from the various film and cartoon versions of *A Christmas Carol* showing the children Ignorance and Want at **www.cedmagic.com**. Type 'Ignorance and Want' into the search engine on the website.

The Ghost is visibly older and says his time is almost finished. However, before he leaves Scrooge asks about a strange object he sees sticking out of the bottom of his robe. It looks like a claw but it is in fact the bony foot of a small, skeletal child. The ghost reveals two such children, a boy, called Ignorance, and a girl, called Want. They are so malnourished they look near death. Their 'stale and shrivelled' (Stave Three, p. 73) condition brings to mind a piece of bread or fruit with all its goodness withered away. Dickens' disturbing description likens the children to clawed devils when they should be angels. The contrast from the jovial atmosphere of

Christmas cheer we have seen in the rest of this Stave is particularly forceful and makes us take notice.

The Ghost tells Scrooge that these children are the creation of 'Man' (Stave Three, p. 73), using 'Man' to refer to men and women, or society. Dickens' message broadens here: it is not just Scrooge the Ghost is addressing but mankind in general, including ourselves. We are told to 'beware of ... both' (Stave Three, p. 73) these children, but especially to beware of 'Ignorance'. This might seem the wrong way round at first, for surely 'Want', or need, must be addressed; if people are without food and shelter they cannot survive. However, the warning of the dangers of Ignorance links to Dickens' belief in the need for education, to eradicate Want through knowledge.

The power of education

Dickens believed that only through education could the cycle of poverty be broken. Through allowing poor people better access to well-paid jobs and by giving them the confidence and knowledge to progress in life, Dickens believed that education was the route out of poverty, crime and despair. He makes this point powerfully in this **novella**. His introduction of the child characters of 'Ignorance' and 'Want' is an example of the direct social message he is trying to convey. It could also be said that Scrooge is undergoing his own education — learning to see the consequences of his actions. Scrooge's 'ignorance' is a direct cause of the Cratchits 'want' and he must learn from this knowledge.

STAVE FOUR: THE LAST OF THE SPIRITS

[PP. 74–83] – A MAN HAS DIED

1 The Ghost of Christmas Yet to Come appears. It does not speak, but points the way.

2 Businessmen in the City discuss a colleague who has died; they don't care about his death.

DID YOU KNOW?

Dickens was a strong believer in the power of education and persuaded his friend, the wealthy Angela Burdett-Coutts, to provide financial support for the Ragged Schools (see **Setting and background**). Dickens made many recommendations such as to provide soap and water for the children to clean themselves.

❸ Thieves meet to sell items they have stolen from the dead man.

❹ A young couple are given hope that they will have longer to repay a loan because this man has died.

This last Ghost is more sinister than the previous ones. It is described as a 'Phantom' (Stave Four, p. 74) and the use of three adverbs to clarify its arrival slows the pace and establishes a graver, more solemn tone: it 'slowly, gravely, silently approached'. The Ghost does not wear the festive robe its two predecessors did but is 'shrouded' (Stave Four, p. 74) in black, thus alluding to death by calling to mind visions of the 'Grim Reaper'. It is surrounded in darkness and can hardly be seen; indeed Scrooge feels its presence rather than sees it. This Ghost doesn't speak, but points the way Scrooge must go. Scrooge provides the commentary for us here, sharing his conclusion that we are going to see shadows of what might be if events continue as they are.

CHECKPOINT 23

How is this Ghost different to Scrooge's previous supernatural visitors?

We see a changed Scrooge even before he is exposed to the sights the Ghost has in store for him. Scrooge is nervous and can hardly stand. He finds it very unnerving that the Ghost can look at him but he can't see the Ghost. However, he understands that he needs to learn the lessons he is about to receive. This is a very different character from the one we first met; he has already resolved to 'live to be another man from what I was' (Stave Four, p. 75) and we wonder why he has to see what this Ghost is about to show him.

Scrooge is first taken to a group of businessmen in the City of London, by the Exchange, where Scrooge himself works. The Ghost stops in order to overhear their conversation about a colleague who has recently died. This conversation is shocking because of the indifference with which they speak of the dead man. They wonder why he died and what he did with his money. Their concern is merely self-interest – will there be a good lunch at the funeral? If so they will attend. There is no concern for a life that is over; it will not affect these men in the slightest. A second group of men confirm the death of 'old Scratch' (Stave Four, p. 76) with a similar lack of emotion; they mention his death and then talk about the weather.

Scrooge articulates our wonder at these conversations and feels 'assured that they must have some hidden purpose' (Stave Four, p. 77). He cannot think who they are speaking of, but realises that it will probably become clear. Providing Scrooge and the reader with a mystery in the form of a set of clues to solve is a typical part of ghost stories and helps to engage us. We are, perhaps, faster than Scrooge in realising the dead man they are speaking of is him; he doesn't realise the significance of his absence from 'his accustomed corner' (Stave Four, p. 77), hoping it means that he has managed to change his life, as he intends to. We realise that these scenes are indicators of what will happen if he doesn't change; if Scrooge wants to have an impact on the world and be remembered he must act positively.

Scrooge and the Ghost go into a poorer part of the town that has a bad reputation. The adjectives are piled up to create an overwhelming sense of despair and horror: the streets are 'foul and narrow; the shops and houses wretched; the people half naked, drunken, slipshod, ugly' (Stave Four, p. 77), the smells are bad and 'the whole quarter reeked with crime, with filth, and misery' (Stave Four, p. 77). Like many social reformers, Dickens believed that crime is often a result of poverty and misery.

Three people, a 'charwoman', a 'laundress', and an 'undertaker's man' (Stave Four, p. 78) enter a dark and dirty shop. They have brought items to sell to old Joe, the man who runs this shop. They recognise each other because they have all stolen their items from the dead man. They justify their actions as taking care of themselves, as the dead man always did, and don't see that anyone has suffered from their thefts – the man died without anyone to care for him or miss him or his possessions. Although on face value these claims might seem logical, the attitudes of the people shock us because they are so harsh and uncaring, in the same way that Scrooge's cruel sentiments about the poor could be seen, in certain lights, to make economic sense (Stave One, pp. 17–18).

Scrooge's reaction is horror; he shudders, identifying with the plight of the dead man who has lived his life in a similar manner to him,

CHECK THE BOOK

Crime was on the increase in the growing Victorian cities. Dickens describes street crime memorably in *Oliver Twist*.

CHECKPOINT 24

Why have these people stolen these goods?

GLOSSARY

slipshod to be careless or sloppy

charwoman someone who is employed to do housework

laundress a woman who takes in and does washing for others

undertaker's man someone who works for an undertaker

but does not yet realise that it is his future self they are talking about.

The scene changes and Scrooge sees the corpse of the man, 'plundered and bereft, unwatched, unwept, uncared for' (Stave Four, p. 81). The Ghost points to the covered head and although Scrooge could draw back the sheet and see the face he does not have the courage to do so. In a moment of heightened suspense, the Ghost points again, but still Scrooge will not look.

Scrooge is so shaken by the callous and uncaring way this man has been treated in death he asks to see anyone who feels emotion at the man's passing. He is shown a young couple who are emotional, but it is not the emotion he is expecting. The husband is 'careworn and depressed, though he was young' (Stave Four, p. 83) and he is ashamed of the natural relief he feels at the news he has heard. The dead man had lent them money but they were having difficulty in paying it back and needed more time, something the man had refused. The husband had gone to see him, one final time, to ask for an extension, but found that the man had died. Now the debt will be passed to another lender, but this will take time, enabling the couple to save more money. As a consequence, the news of the man's death is good for them – it saves them from financial disaster. We realise this is a good-hearted couple as they are ashamed and embarrassed by their response to the man's death, but his demise nevertheless gives them hope.

DID YOU KNOW?

Dickens knew the full horror of debt, having seen his father thrown into prison as a result of his debts. As a child he had to sell the family possessions or take them to the pawnbroker. He vowed never to let himself get into that position and wouldn't stop working, even when his doctors warned him to slow down.

What good is money when you're dead?

These scenes illustrate the sentiments voiced by Fred in Stave Three – money is only of use if you do good with it. Scrooge is a rich man who hoards his money for himself, but the Ghost shows him how his money will be of no use to him when he is dead. In fact, in this Stave, Scrooge's money is shown to be a target for the thieves, who justify their actions with reference to his meanness. It also becomes a point of discussion for his ex-colleagues who only want to know what had happened to it, and care nothing for Scrooge as a man at all.

[PP. 84–6] – THE DEATH OF TINY TIM

1 The Cratchits are distraught because Tiny Tim has died.

2 Fred has offered to help if he can.

3 They all resolve to remember the goodness of Tiny Tim and take comfort from it.

This famous scene provides a stark contrast with the death we have seen already in this Stave. Tiny Tim's death is foreshadowed by the Ghost, for if things do not change, he will die. The energetic, boisterous family we joined for Christmas in the previous Stave are now 'Quiet. Very quiet' (Stave Four, p. 84) and the children are 'as still as statues' (Stave Four, p. 84). Mrs Cratchit is trying not to cry, and blames the candlelight and her sewing for affecting her eyes. They are all trying to continue, but it is obvious that the loss of Tiny Tim has affected them greatly. They discuss the change in Bob, and the fact he is walking far more slowly than he used to, an indication of his sorrow and distress.

When Bob appears the emotional nature of the scene is increased, to what some might call **over-sentimental**, and we are made to suffer his loss with him. He has been to the graveyard and found a spot for Tim; moreover, he has promised his dead son that he will walk there every Sunday. He breaks down in tears and the narrator excuses this because it shows the bond between him and his son. Bob goes upstairs and sits by the boy's body, gaining comfort from his memories.

When Bob returns downstairs he tells the rest of the family of the kindness of Fred, whom he met in the street. Fred has only asked after Bob and the family, but Bob takes this as the greatest kindness, reminding us of Dickens' message that it is just as important to look out for one another and provide emotional support as it is to give financial aid.

Bob turns the family's grief into support and consolation by reminding them of Tiny Tim and promising that they should not

GLOSSARY

plundered to loot or steal everything of value

bereft a form of the word 'bereave', meaning to be deprived of or without

forget him. He proposes using the qualities of Tiny Tim to help them become better people, and we see them as a strong family unit.

Sentimental or essential?

Some critics have accused this scene of being too **sentimental** whilst others see it as essential to the novella. Whenever Dickens read it on tour it was guaranteed to make people use their handkerchiefs to dry their tears, and it is said this is the response he wanted. The power of literature to arouse feelings of pity or sorrow is called **pathos** and comes from the Greek word for suffering. It is a shared suffering that Dickens is aiming at here: he wants his readers to feel involved in the story. Although this scene might seem overly sentimental today, it is typical of Victorian literature and is an important contrast to the ending of the novella, as it shows us what could have been if Scrooge didn't change his ways.

[PP. 86–8] – SCROOGE'S GRAVESTONE

1. Scrooge realises that he must face the part he played in the scenes the Ghost has shown him and asks who the dead man was.

2. Scrooge sees a different man working in his office.

3. Scrooge is shown a gravestone with his name on it and realises he is the dead man.

4. He vows to change.

Scrooge is filled with dread and finally faces up to what the reader has already deduced. He asks who the dead man is. The Ghost does not speak but shows him his office and a gravestone.

Scrooge hasn't worked out that the scenes shown by the Ghost of Christmas Yet to Come are what will happen if the present remains unchanged. Because he has already vowed to change he thinks he will be able to see the new, improved, Scrooge. He recognises his

office and asks to look in, to 'behold what I shall be in days to come' (Stave Four, p. 87). This lack of understanding means that when Scrooge realises he is the unloved and unmissed dead man the horror of it is even greater. Scrooge looks in his office window and sees that the furniture is different and someone else is working there. The narrator doesn't comment on what this means, but the reader works it out before Scrooge does.

The Ghost takes Scrooge to a churchyard and Scrooge realises he is about to learn the name of the 'wretched man' (Stave Four, p. 87). It is overgrown with grass and weeds, not cared-for as we know Tiny Tim's grave will be. Scrooge gets increasingly nervous and asks if these 'shadows' (Stave Four, p. 87) he is seeing are certain or may be changed – he is starting to guess the truth although he is not able to articulate it yet. These questions and the Ghost's refusal to say anything help to build up the suspense and make the revelation of the name on the gravestone even more dramatic. When Scrooge reads his name on the gravestone he falls to his knees, horrified at what his future currently holds. It is the final jolt he needs to transform himself forever. Scrooge promises to change his ways so he may 'sponge away the writing on this stone!' (Stave Four, p. 88). The shock and horror has been so great for him that we believe he truly means what he says.

CHECKPOINT 25

Why is the gravestone such a shock to Scrooge?

Scrooge tries to hold the Ghost's hand but it won't let him. However, his despair and desperation to know how he can change the future he has been shown means he manages to hold the Ghost for a little while. He isn't successful for long and the struggle is won by the Ghost who is stronger than Scrooge. With both hands free Scrooge puts them together in prayer and sees the Ghost's shape change until it disappears and he is looking at his own bedpost.

Stave Five: The End of It

[pp. 89–93] – Scrooge wakes on Christmas Day

1 Scrooge wakes and finds everything as he left it.

2 He is overwhelmed at having a chance to put things right and delighted at everything he sees.

3 He arranges for a prize turkey to be sent to the Cratchits.

4 On his way to church he makes a large donation to the Charity Collectors he sent away the day before.

The atmosphere and tone of this Stave is hugely different to the preceding one, showing us the extent of Scrooge's changed character. The short exclamations that make up the narration and **dialogue** help to create a sense of joy and wonder and underpin Scrooge's happiness at being given a second chance. He can hardly speak because he is so excited. He delights in all he sees, from the bed curtains, which are not torn down, to the saucepan in which he had cooked his gruel. Humour is created in the description of him putting his clothes on inside out and upside down and by Scrooge's language. He uses a string of **similes**, 'as light as a feather … as happy as an angel … as merry as a schoolboy … as giddy as a drunken man' (Stave Five, p. 90); these light and airy images capture his emotions vividly and emphasise the extent of his changed nature. He now revels in these feelings whereas he would have rejected and condemned them in the first Stave.

Scrooge starts laughing, reminding us of Fred's constant good humour, and we are told this is the first of much more laughter to come; it is 'the father of a long, long line of brilliant laughs' (Stave Five, p. 90). He is such a different person he realises he doesn't even know what day it is, indeed he feels he doesn't know anything about the world anymore. For Scrooge this is the equivalent of a rebirth: 'I'm quite a baby' (Stave Five, p. 90), he says. This relates to the Christian concept of being born again when the path of Christ is accepted, and reminds us that the Christian religion allows all past sins to be forgiven when you repent of them and try not to repeat them. This means that Scrooge's past wrong-doings are forgiven and he is able to start again. The religious significance of his statement is underlined by the bells of the church ringing, 'Clash, clash, hammer; ding, dong, bell!' (Stave Five, p. 90).

The contrast between this Scrooge and the first one we met is further highlighted by the changed weather. **Pathetic fallacy** is employed once again to show us Scrooge's new 'sunny disposition': the fog and mist has gone. Now it is 'clear, bright, jovial, stirring, cold; cold, piping for the blood to dance to; golden sunlight; heavenly sky; sweet fresh air; merry bells' (Stave Five, p. 90). This list coveys a wonderfully positive atmosphere, a real contrast to the opening of the novella, and shows how the same setting can be transformed.

> **CHECKPOINT 26**
>
> How does the weather reflect Scrooge's transformation?

Scrooge is given the opportunity to put right some of the wrongs he committed the previous day, on Christmas Eve. He first encounters a young boy (in a parallel to the carol singer he chased away) and Scrooge has to ask what day it is. Scrooge is delighted to hear it is Christmas Day, realising the Ghosts' visits all took place in one night. This is something we have to accept, just like all the other supernatural events in the story (see **Theme** on the **Supernatural**).

Scrooge asks the boy to go and buy the big prize turkey that was hanging in the poulterer's window and offers to pay him for doing so. We see how generous his offer must be from the boy's response: he was 'off like a shot' (Stave Five, p. 91). Scrooge intends to send the turkey to the Cratchits but doesn't want them to know who sent it. The fact he doesn't want recognition or thanks for this deed tells us he is doing it for the Cratchits rather than for himself – a big change in him.

CHECK THE NET

On the British Library's website you can find a page from Mrs Beeton's cookbook of 1859 about the Christmas turkey. Mrs Beeton was one of the most famous cookery writers of the nineteenth century. Go to **www.bl.uk** and type 'christmas turkey' into the search engine.

Scrooge goes downstairs and waits for the turkey to be brought to him; as he waits he notices the door knocker and claims he shall 'love it as long as I live' (Stave Five, p. 91). This shows us that he is not acting differently out of fear, but welcomes his new way of life and is enjoying it. It is important we see that acting in this way is more satisfying and rewarding than being selfish; Scrooge is actually benefiting from this change. When the turkey arrives his generosity continues and he pays for it to be delivered by cab, laughing as he spends all this money.

Scrooge continues to get ready to go out, even though he is too excited to shave – 'his hand continued to shake' (Stave Five, p. 92) – and he can't stop dancing. Putting on his best clothes he goes out and sees people in the streets in the manner shown by the Ghost of Christmas Present. He smiles at everyone so much that a few people wish him a 'merry Christmas!' (Stave Five, p. 92), something that he is so pleased by he starts saying it to others.

He sees one of the Charity Collectors he was so rude to the previous day and feels 'a pang across his heart' (Stave Five, p. 92), remembering how he behaved and what this man must think of him. However, he decides he has to put right his wrongs immediately and goes to the gentleman to ask his pardon and offer a large sum of money. Not only does he give what might be expected for this year, but includes 'back-payments' (Stave Five, p. 93) to make up for his mean and selfish years. Once again, Scrooge rejects thanks, showing he sees this charity as his duty.

[PP. 93–4] – CHRISTMAS AT FRED'S

❶ Scrooge goes to Fred's and asks if he can join him for Christmas after all.

❷ He is welcomed and they have a wonderful Christmas together.

Scrooge spends the morning at church and then walks around the city, gaining pleasure from all that he sees. In the afternoon he walks to Fred's house, to accept the offer of spending Christmas with him that he so rudely rejected the day before. He is nervous about going in and walks up and down the pavement outside the house before having the courage to knock at the door. This shows us that part of the change in Scrooge is a new concern about how others feel, something he did not care about before.

Scrooge is welcomed into the house with joy – 'it is a mercy [Fred] didn't shake his arm off' (Stave Five, p. 94) – and we are told that he 'was at home in five minutes' (Stave Five, p. 94). The other guests that Scrooge saw with the Ghost join them and they have a 'wonderful' day (Stave Five, p. 94). In fact, 'wonderful' is repeated four times to emphasise this point.

> **CHECKPOINT 27**
>
> What is the effect of 'wonderful' (Stave Five, p. 94) being repeated so often?

[PP. 94–5] – HELPING THE CRATCHITS

❶ Scrooge is at the office early on Boxing Day.

❷ He raises Bob's salary and offers to help Tiny Tim and the family.

❸ Scrooge gains a reputation for being a generous and good man.

❹ Tiny Tim survives.

The next morning Scrooge is desperate to see Bob Cratchit in order that he can organise to help him and his family and so arrives at the office early. Bob is late, as would be traditional for workers on Boxing Day, but he is very nervous about this as the Scrooge he knows would have been extremely angry. As a sign of how much Scrooge has changed he plays a joke on Bob, and tries to act as he used to, growling 'in his accustomed voice as near as he could feign it' (Stave Five, p. 94). Scrooge can't even speak as he used to as his whole being is too full of laughter and happiness. He isn't able to keep up the joke for long and tells Bob he is going to raise his salary, a statement that is so unlike Scrooge Bob can't quite understand it; he actually thinks Scrooge must have gone mad and he will have to call for 'help and a strait-waistcoat' (Stave Five, p. 94).

Typical of this sort of fiction, the novella now races to an end. Once it is established that Scrooge is now a transformed character we are told of all the good deeds he does and time moves swiftly forward.

> **GLOSSARY**
>
> **feign** to pretend or deceive
>
> **strait-waistcoat** now known as a strait-jacket, a garment where the arms went into long sleeves that then were tied round the body to restrain the wearer

DID YOU KNOW?

Dickens forgot to tell us Tiny Tim's fate in the first draft and added it to the manuscript as it was going to the printers!

We are already convinced that Scrooge will change his ways so do not need to know the full details of his actions. Being told he 'was better than his word' (Stave Five, p. 95) allows us to imagine how he helps the Cratchits even more than he promised. The key point in all of this, which emphasises the change in Scrooge, is the fact that Tiny Tim 'did *not* die' (Stave Five, p. 95). Instead, Scrooge becomes a second father to him, a term that is reminiscent of God's position as 'holy father' in Christian belief.

We are left with a comforting and rounded picture of this changed man; the term 'good' is used to describe him many times, a technique that emphasises his new character. Even though 'some people laughed to see the alteration in him' (Stave Five, p. 95) he does not care, showing his belief and commitment to his new life. Indeed, he now values laughter so much he prefers they laugh at him than don't laugh at all. All he wants is for his own heart to laugh, which it does.

We are left with the narrator's summary of him as a man who was regarded as knowing 'how to keep Christmas well' (Stave Five, p. 95) and who never saw ghosts again. This suggests that he did not dwell on his past mistakes but embraced his new life. We are left with Tiny Tim's famous words, 'God bless Us, Every One!' (Stave Five, p. 95) to remind us of the Christian message of this story. Concluding with Tiny Tim's words reminds us that Scrooge saved him, and that this small boy represents life and hope for us all.

> **Wrapping up the story**
>
> The events proceed faster and faster in this final Stave, showing how life races by for Scrooge once it is full of happiness and the friendship of other people. We are left with a clear impression of a reformed and happy human being.

CHECKPOINT 28

Why has Dickens
written this
novella? What is
his message?

Now take a break!

WHO SAYS ...?

1 'keep Christmas in your own way, and let me keep it in mine.'

....

2 'I wear the chain I forged in life'

....

3 'A small matter ... to make these silly folks so full of gratitude.'

....

5 'A great many back-payments are included in it, I assure you.'

....

4 'His wealth is of no use to him. He don't do any good with it.'

....

ABOUT WHOM?

6 'brave in ribbons'

....

7 'but most of all beware this boy'

....

8 'he knew how to keep Christmas well'

....

Check your answers on p. 119.

GENERAL SUMMARY: 'THE POOR RELATION'S STORY'

PAGES 114–18: MICHAEL'S FAILED LIFE?

Michael, the narrator, is the 'poor relation' of the story. He has been invited to John Spatter's house on Christmas Day and is asked to tell a story to the family and friends gathered round the fire.

He starts by summarising what these people must think of him – he has failed in his business, failed in love and failed his uncle, who expected more of him. He now lives in a rented room on Clapham Road where he has to be out during the day and stays in bed in the evening because he cannot afford heating. To fill his days, Michael visits people he used to work with, drinks coffee and takes his cousin's son, Little Frank, out. He is very fond of this child.

Michael then moves on to tell his audience that this picture they have of him is wrong and he actually lives in a Castle.

PAGES 118–25: MICHAEL'S 'CASTLE'

Although the gathered company think John Spatter took his business from him, Michael says this is not the case and they are still successful business partners and good friends. Michael lives in the Castle with his loving wife, Christiana, who went against her mother's wishes in order to marry him.

Michael's children are all grown up and his eldest daughter has married John Spatter's son. Michael spends happy evenings at the Castle surrounded by his children and grandchildren, with Christiana at the piano.

This whole picture is brought crashing down at the end of the story, when Michael reveals his 'Castle' is an imaginary place he retreats to when his real life becomes too sad for him. The way the others see him – as a failure, lonely, poor and downtrodden – is in fact the real truth of Michael's life.

 DID YOU KNOW?

This story is one of two Dickens wrote for the Christmas edition of the journal *Household Words* (1852). They made part of a larger collection called 'A Round of Stories by the Christmas Fire'.

CHECKPOINT 29

Why does Michael have to 'fill his days out'?

CHECKPOINT 30

What is it about Christmas time that means Michael mentally retreats to his 'Castle'?

DETAILED SUMMARIES: 'THE POOR RELATION'S STORY'

[PP. 114–18] – MICHAEL'S FAILED LIFE?

❶ Michael, the poor relation, tells a story at Christmas.

❷ We learn that he was a failure in business and in love and was rejected by his Uncle Chill.

❸ He now lives a mundane life, on very little money and his only happiness is to spend time with his nephew, Little Frank.

❹ To our astonishment, Michael then says that all this is false and that he in fact lives in a Castle.

The story starts with an **omniscient narrator** explaining how Michael, the poor relation, comes to be telling a story. A group of family members sit in a 'goodly circle' around the fire at Christmas for the telling of traditional stories. Michael is 'very reluctant' (p. 114) to start the story-telling as he feels that everyone else is more important than he is and that they should tell their stories first. Michael singles out John, 'our esteemed host' (p. 114) in particular. However, the guests call out in encouragement, and he prepares to begin.

From the second paragraph Michael takes over the narration. We, as readers, become like one of the Christmas guests around the fire. This has the effect of drawing us into the story but it will also make us think about how we respond to characters such as Michael as his story proceeds. It is worth remembering that at least one of the people mentioned in his story is present to hear it.

Once again, Michael is very polite, calling John 'our esteemed host' for the second time and complimenting him on his hospitality. However, he tells his audience that the story he is about to relate will surprise them, especially John. This makes us intrigued and want to read on.

After telling us he is 'not what I am supposed to be' (p. 115), Michael says he will outline the image the family has of him. He sums himself up as 'nobody's enemy but my own' (p. 115), meaning he is seen as someone who has brought about his own bad fortune.

Michael tells us that his failure in business is generally held to be a result of his 'unbusiness-like and incredulous' (p. 115) attitude, by which he allowed his business partner, John Spatter, the host of this gathering, to deceive him and take over his business. This seems to be a very strange thing to say, especially in the light of the compliments he earlier paid to John. This makes us start to realise that all is not as it seems with this man, or his story.

The next thing Michael discusses is his apparent failure in love. Once again he describes how he was deceived by someone, this time by his sweetheart Christiana. 'I was ridiculously trustful', he says (p. 115). Following this he mentions failing his Uncle Chill by 'not being as sharp as he could have wished in worldly matters', in other words, being naïve in business and in his dealings with other people. The name Uncle Chill sounds so disapproving and heartless we already start to get an idea of this character.

Michael is living on a small allowance and implies he can't mention the amount because it would embarrass John. As the story continues we wonder if the reason for the embarrassment might be due to the small, rather than generous, nature of this allowance.

CHECKPOINT 31

What is your initial impression of Michael?

GLOSSARY
incredulous
unbelieving, naïve

Double meanings

Much of what Michael says can have two meanings. When he describes his failed life he says that this is how he is 'supposed' to live, not how he actually lives. This allows him to suggest that his real life is something different, but also makes the reader think about how Michael has been judged by other people. It becomes clear that the family 'suppose' the worst in him and blame him for his misfortunes. The fact that Michael makes a point of complimenting John could therefore be seen as **ironic**, given that John tricked Michael out of his business.

Michael's daily routine is outlined. The conditions he lives in would have been typical of someone in his situation. He rents a room in a house in Clapham Road, 'a very clean back room, in a very respectable house' (p. 115) but is not allowed to use it during the day unless he is unwell. As modern readers we would probably be appalled by this, and this seems to be the response Dickens wants. The matter-of-fact tone used here is a clever way of provoking a reaction. As a result of not being allowed to use his room in the daytime, Michael has to 'get through the day' (p. 115), something that isn't easy to do if you have very little money. He outlines his day in precise detail, suggesting that it is rather boring and mundane. By including all the costs he reminds us that he has to count every penny. When he returns to his room he has to get into the bed as he can't afford to light the fire. Even that is 'objected to by the family on account of its giving trouble and making a dirt' (p. 116). Once again the matter-of-fact tone passes no direct comment but leaves us to react to the situation.

CHECKPOINT 32

Michael is paying rent on this room. Is this treatment of him fair?

Our sympathy for Michael is increased when he describes the times he gets invited for a meal at the house of a friend or relative as 'holiday occasions' (p. 115). This suggests these invitations do not happen very often, but he appreciates them greatly when they do. As we have become part of Michael's audience we might start thinking of relatives or friends of our own who might be in similar situations.

Michael moves on to talk of the son of a cousin of his; Little Frank. He is clearly deeply attached to this child who appears to be the only human being to give him love. He wants to leave Frank the only possession he owns, a picture Michael has of himself as a child, in the hope Frank will remember him. Speaking of his own death in this way, Michael makes his situation stark: he has nothing of value to leave and because of this isn't valued by his family.

The story then changes pace and tone. Michael clears his throat and raises the volume of his voice, clear indications that he is going to reveal something important. He tells us that all we have heard of him so far 'is the general impression about me' (p. 117) and that this impression is wrong. Not only is this not his life, but the routines he has described are not his either. This is confusing at first and it is only at the end of the story that we realise the truth of what he is saying.

Michael says he in fact does not live in Clapham Road, adding, 'Comparatively speaking, I am very seldom there. I reside, mostly, in a … Castle' (p. 117). This is a real surprise to the reader – a Castle is so far removed from the rented room we believed he lived in. However, the words he uses are very specific – he says this residence is not a Castle in the 'old baronial' sense although everyone would agree that it is a Castle, and that he is 'seldom' at Clapham Road – this means that he is there sometimes.

[PP. 118–25] – MICHAEL'S 'CASTLE'

① Michael describes his happy and fulfilled life, the opposite of the one described in the first part of the story.

② He is successful in business and happily married, with a loving family.

③ However, Michael eventually reveals that this is an illusion and not real.

④ He needs his 'Castle' and illusionary life to help him cope with the harsh reality of his own existence.

CHECKPOINT 33

How do you think the guests sitting round the fire might be reacting to Michael's story?

GLOSSARY

baronial in a style that is suitable for a baron (the lowest member of the British nobility)

Once Michael has dropped this bombshell he goes on to re-tell his story, and it is a very different story from the one previously outlined. He tells us that when he was twenty-five he had his own business although he was still living with his Uncle Chill. John Spatter was his clerk but Michael made him a partner in the business. At this time he also proposed to, and was accepted by, his sweetheart Christiana. This changes everything we had thought about him and Michael goes on to elaborate.

CHECKPOINT 34

Why does Uncle Chill disapprove of Christiana?

Michael was deeply in love with Christiana and didn't mind the fact she didn't have any money but he knew his rich Uncle Chill wouldn't approve. His uncle's behaviour lives up to his name. Like Scrooge in *A Christmas Carol*, Uncle Chill is a mean-spirited man whose cold nature is reflected in the freezing temperature of his house: Michael notices it is 'colder in my uncle's unwarmed house than in the street' (p. 118). The description of his Uncle's domestic help, Betsy Snap, 'a withered, hard-favoured, yellow old woman' (p. 119), makes the scene even harsher as the two stare disapprovingly at Michael. Uncle Chill decides Christiana just wants to marry Michael to get her hands on his, Uncle's Chill's, fortune when he dies. Uncle Chill says he will 'spoil the speculation' (p. 120). This word is associated with gambling and the stock-market and suggests that Christiana's mother and Uncle Chill view the marriage proposal only in financial terms.

Michael tells him that Christiana is not after Uncle Chill's money. Instead Michael believes she only wants to marry him for 'pure, disinterested, faithful love' (p. 120). The language of this claim does seem rather excessive, making us worry about Christiana's motives. Michael and Uncle Chill go to see Christiana and her mother, at which point Uncle Chill disowns Michael, who never sees him again.

We are told that Christiana does not reject Michael at this point and marry a rich man, but the detail that is included – that the dirt from the wheels on her carriage often splatters Michael – seems strange to add if it isn't true. Even the use of negatives is a warning sign: 'No, no. She married me' (p. 121). We have no choice but to believe him, but a little seed of doubt has been sewn.

Michael tells us that Christiana 'would rather share [his] struggles than look on' (p. 121) and they go to live in the Castle for 'it dates from that time' (p. 121). They have children who have all been born in it, their eldest being a girl also called Christiana who is now married with a son 'so like Little Frank' (p. 121). This story seems to be a tale of love and solidarity, but the clues are in the language. Once we know the ending of the story we can start to read this information in a different light.

Reality and fantasy

Once we know the imaginary nature of Michael's 'Castle' we can piece together the clues from the earlier narrative. As life gets harsher for Michael he creates this imaginary 'Castle' in which to escape. It is significant therefore that we are told that the 'Castle' dates from the time of his marriage to Christiana, or, as we find out later, the time at which she rejected him and all his hopes of family life were dashed. Here we have two possible stories running alongside each other: the one harsh reality and the other perfect fantasy.

Michael now turns his attention to his business dealings, telling his audience that any stories they might have heard about John treating him 'coldly, as a poor simpleton' (p. 122) when he was trying to deal with the consequences of his Uncle's actions are wrong. He says John did not treat him in this way, 'nor did he afterwards gradually possess himself of our business and edge me out' (p. 122). Again the use of negatives here suggests the truth behind Michael's seemingly mild words. He is being very clever here, telling his audience, which includes John, exactly what happened but at the same time denying it. Michael relays a long conversation with John where they discuss the many ways Michael helped him in the past. The **irony** is heightened as John is shown as being grateful, 'his face glowing with friendship' (p. 123). John is shown supposedly recalling how Michael has supported him, while at the same time, we realise, preparing to cheat Michael out of his own business. As with Christiana, Michael creates for himself a much happier alternative where John treats him with respect.

GLOSSARY
disinterested unselfish and without self-interest

CHECKPOINT 35

Why does knowing the possible happy outcome make the actual unhappy outcome worse?

At this point, as we are starting to wonder whether Michael is living in the Castle at all, he draws together some of its benefits: the Castle 'has a warm and cheerful air, and is quite a picture of Home' (p. 124). The terms 'air' and 'picture' also seem to hint about the reality of the Castle but Michael is so calm and certain in his narration he is difficult to doubt.

Michael tells us he does not know what loneliness is in his Castle; his wife is always there and she often sings to him. At this particular time of year, i.e., Christmas, he is 'seldom' ever out of it (p. 124). Michael finally reveals that his Castle isn't real at all but an imaginary retreat from the harsh realities of his life. The truth is that Christiana did refuse to marry him, choosing a rich man instead, and John did deceive him out of his business. Instead of the Castle, he does live in a rented room.

> ### The ending
> The ending comes as a painful shock, even though the imaginary nature of the Castle has been hinted at throughout the story. Michael has seemed a very balanced and mild narrator and wholly unlikely to make up such a fantasy. It is at this point we start looking back at the story and wondering why he needed to invent and live in a fantasy home. The answer can be found in the behaviour of those around him and the uncaring ways that society at large treats unfortunate people such as Michael. Here Dickens conveys the power of the individual imagination whilst making a social comment.

'THE POOR RELATION'S STORY'

CHECKPOINT 36

Why does Michael need the 'Castle'? What does this tell us of conditions of the time?

Now take a break!

Who says ...?

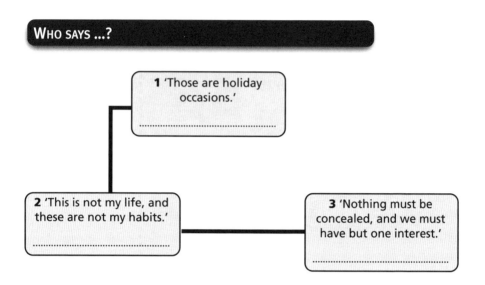

1 'Those are holiday occasions.'

....

2 'This is not my life, and these are not my habits.'

....

3 'Nothing must be concealed, and we must have but one interest.'

....

About whom?

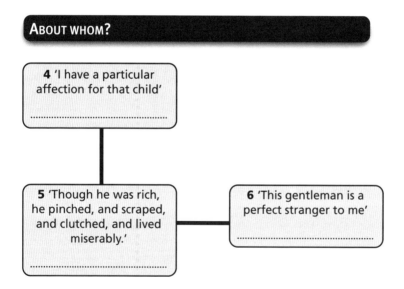

4 'I have a particular affection for that child'

....

5 'Though he was rich, he pinched, and scraped, and clutched, and lived miserably.'

....

6 'This gentleman is a perfect stranger to me'

....

Check your answers on p. 119.

GENERAL SUMMARY: 'THE SIGNALMAN'

PAGES 105–10: DESCENDING INTO HELL

The narrator is out walking when he sees a Signalman in his signal box. It is situated at the bottom of a railway cutting, by the entrance to a tunnel. He calls down to the Signalman who responds with shock and horror.

The narrator makes his way down to the signal box – it is like descending into hell or a coffin – and talks to the Signalman. He learns that the Signalman spends his lonely hours educating himself. The Signalman regrets not working harder at university and not achieving any qualifications.

The Signalman does his job with care as they talk, except twice he looks at the warning bell and the tunnel entrance when there is no warning or train. The narrator finds this strange and the Signalman agrees to tell his story the next night.

PAGES 110–18: THE SPECTRE'S WARNING

The next night, when the narrator returns, the Signalman explains that he is troubled as he has heard the warning bell ring and a voice cry out a warning at the tunnel entrance. He has even seen an apparition, a spectre, waving at him one moment, and gone the next.

The first time this happened he checked to see if there was a problem but was told all was fine. Six hours later there was an awful train crash in the tunnel and many people were killed and injured. Six or seven months later he saw the spectre at the tunnel entrance again; following this appearance a young woman died on the train as it went past his box. He now fears that a third terrible event will happen.

The narrator inspects the warning light and bell but can't see anything wrong with them. He tries to comfort the Signalman and then leaves for the night. When he returns the next day, he finds the Signalman is dead, having been run over by a train coming out of the tunnel. The Signalman did not respond to the warning given by the train driver, who waved and covered his eyes just as the spectre had done.

 DID YOU KNOW?

When this story was originally published it was called 'No. 1 Branch Line. The Signalman'.

CHECKPOINT 37

The Signalman does his job with care. What does this suggest about his ability and reliability? Is he the sort of person to imagine seeing ghosts?

DETAILED SUMMARIES: 'THE SIGNALMAN'

[PP. 105–10] – DESCENDING INTO HELL

1 The narrator is out walking and sees a Signalman, at the bottom of a railway cutting, by a tunnel.

2 The Signalman acts very strangely when the narrator calls down to him.

3 The narrator climbs down to talk with him.

4 The Signalman is very cagey at first and doesn't reveal why he was disturbed by the narrator's appearance.

5 He promises that if the narrator returns the next night he will tell him the cause of his distress.

The story starts with a call, 'Halloa! Below there!' (p. 105). This form of 'hello' is used to call out a greeting and suggests the speaker is trying to project his voice a long way. The Signalman obviously hears this call but instead of looking up to the top of the cutting he looks towards the entrance of the tunnel. This strange opening immediately attracts our attention as, along with the narrator, we want to find out why he does this.

CHECK THE BOOK

Try reading the other stories from Dickens' collection of 1866 to get a clearer picture of the narrator and the themes that unite them.

> ### The narrator
>
> This short story is actually part of a series called 'Mugby Junction'. These stories were originally published in the 1866 Christmas issue of a journal called *All the Year Round*. All the stories are narrated by one character, Mr Jackson. He used to work for a firm called Barbox Brothers and, although he did very well, he is not happy and takes a train to run away from his birthday. He gets out at Mugby Junction by chance and finds friends there, especially Phoebe, who is unwell and not able to get out of bed. He explores Mugby Junction so he can tell her stories about what he has seen. 'The Signalman' is the story of one of his investigations. If you read this story on its own, which many people do, you don't find out the narrator's name or why he is there. To reflect this, Mr Jackson is referred to as 'the narrator' throughout this Note.

The narrator describes the Signalman's actions and the setting with precision; the figure is 'foreshortened and shadowed, down in the deep trench' (p. 105), which reminds the reader of looking down into a grave. The atmosphere is oppressive and threatening, even the sunset is 'angry' (p. 105). The strange behaviour, the shadows and the sunset, suggesting night is about to fall, are all key ingredients of a ghost story and we start to feel a sense of unease as the narrator decides to climb down to join the Signalman.

The path down is difficult and as he follows it the narrator thinks about the reluctance with which the Signalman pointed it out; he obviously does not welcome visitors. We are also given a detailed description of the setting: there is 'clammy stone, that became oozier and wetter' (p. 106), and at the bottom the 'dripping-wet wall of jagged stone' (p. 106) cuts out 'all view but a strip of sky' (p. 106). This really does feel like the bottom of the earth, and reminds us of a tomb. The narrator emphasises this by telling us 'it had a earthy deadly smell' and that he feels 'as if I had left the natural world' (p. 106). All this helps to create a sinister atmosphere and unsettles us as we read on to see what will happen in this lonely place.

At the bottom of the cutting the huge, dark, gaping mouth of the tunnel dominates the scene. The Signalman's job is to make sure it is

CHECK THE BOOK

Compare this story of the supernatural with another written a couple of years earlier by Amelia B. Edwards. 'The Phantom Coach' first appeared in the 1864 Christmas edition of Dickens' journal *All the Year Round*.

CHECKPOINT 38

Why is the setting described in this way?

safe for an approaching train to go through the tunnel. He is told when a train is coming and is in charge of operating the signals telling it to stop or go. Here, vocabulary such as 'dungeon' and 'terminating' (p. 106), with their associations of imprisonment and death, add to the sense of foreboding we have.

The narrator asks the Signalman about his job but the Signalman is very hesitant and behaves as though he is afraid of him. The Signalman's strange behaviour and pale appearance even make the narrator wonder for a minute if he is looking at a spirit or ghost. The fact that the Signalman himself is afraid dispels this thought however. The Signalman asks the narrator if he has visited him before. This raises our interest and curiosity; we know there is something to find out. Instead of learning what is wrong, we are given lots of detail about the Signalman's job and life. Structuring the story in this way means the reader is engaged and suspense is maintained while lots of background information is provided by the author.

CHECKPOINT 39

What are your first impressions of the Signalman?

The Signalman has many spare hours in his job and has spent them learning another language and improving his mathematics. When he was younger he had gone to university but 'had run wild' (p. 108) and 'misused his opportunities' (p. 108). He appears grimly content, however, as he suggests he has ended up with what he deserved.

The value of education

This passage links with ideas about the value and power of education we have seen in *A Christmas Carol* (see **Setting and background** and the **Detailed summary** on Stave Three, pp. 72–3). Here, however, we have an example of someone who has thrown their chances away. The Signalman is meant to serve as a reminder and warning to the reader. Once he had missed his opportunity for education he 'had gone down, and never risen again' (p. 108).

As the Signalman relays his life story, he is interrupted by having to get up and perform various tasks connected with his job. We learn that in the performance of these tasks he is 'remarkably exact and vigilant' (p. 109). Another strange event occurs however when the Signalman looks towards his alarm bell a couple of times but the narrator is sure that it 'did NOT ring' (p. 109). The capital letters here draw attention to this event; it will be important to the story that the narrator is sure the bell did not sound.

The Signalman confesses that he is troubled by something in particular. As the narrator leaves he arranges to return the next night in order that the Signalman will share his secret with him. The Signalman is insistent, however, that he must not call out when he returns. This is another example of mysterious behaviour on the part of the Signalman, and makes us wonder why he behaves in this way.

[PP. 110–18] – THE SPECTRE'S WARNING

1. The Signalman tells of a strange figure he has seen at the tunnel entrance. It was waving its arms and cried a warning, using the same words the narrator used when he first greeted the Signalman.

2. After this event there was a terrible train crash in the tunnel.

3. Months later there was another fatality when a woman died on a train; this too occurred after the strange figure had appeared.

4. The Signalman knows something else will happen because the spectre has reappeared again. He does not know what to do to prevent it.

5. The narrator tries to reassure him and promises to return the next day.

6. When he returns he finds the Signalman has been killed by a train, despite the driver waving and calling out to him.

7. The words of the narrator when imagining the spectre were used by the train driver before the Signalman's death.

The next night the narrator returns and the Signalman tells him his story. He has seen a strange figure standing in the tunnel entrance. It stands with its left arm covering its face and violently waving its

GLOSSARY
terminating ending

CHECK THE BOOK

Why not try a modern ghost story where a ghostly spectre's appearance foreshadows disaster? *The Woman in Black* by Susan Hill is a good book to compare with 'The Signalman'. It's also a successful stage-play.

WWW. CHECK THE NET

There's a fun website where 'Mr Dickens' has apparently answered students questions about 'The Signalman' and other of his works! Go to **www. talkingto.co.uk**, click on Dickens and then search for 'The Signalman'.

right arm. This is made stranger when he explains that he has also heard the same cry that the narrator used at the beginning of the story, 'Halloa! Below there!' (p. 111). However, the cry has continued with a warning to 'Look out!' (p. 111). What makes this whole story sinister is the fact the figure disappears as the Signalman tries to touch it, suggesting it is a ghost or a spectre.

After seeing the strange figure and hearing its warning, the Signalman checked all was fine by contacting the railway workers up and down the Line from him, and was told all was well.

The narrator wonders whether to believe the Signalman or not. The Signalman's sanity is an important question and we are involved in the narrator's debate over it. The key factor that makes his story believable is that 'within six hours, after the Appearance, the memorable accident on this line happened' (p. 112). The vision now seems to have been a supernatural warning, prefacing a terrible accident, and is made stranger still by the rest of the Signalman's story.

Six or seven months after the accident, the Signalman tells how he saw the spectre again. It didn't call out this time, but 'it leaned against the shaft of the light, with both hands before the face' in 'an action of mourning' (p. 113). Once again the ghost disappeared as the Signalman went up to it. Later in the day, however, he saw 'a confusion of hands and heads' in the window of a passing train. He stopped the train to find 'a beautiful young lady had died instantaneously in one of the compartments' (p. 113).

Following the tradition that disastrous events usually come in threes, we are not surprised to hear the spectre has been back and the bell has been ringing for the past week or so. The Signalman is being haunted frequently by the ghostly visitor and this is the reason the he reacted so strangely when he heard the narrator's first greeting at the beginning of the story. He insisted the narrator did not call out again because he is afraid of the **prophetic** power of these words.

The story gets even stranger when the Signalman reveals that the 'ghost's ring is a strange vibration in the bell' (p. 114) and is not the normal ringing. This explains why, earlier in the story, he was aware of the bell when the narrator was not. The calm and certain way with which the Signalman explains this supernatural activity adds to the sinister atmosphere here and the feeling that something is going to happen.

The Signalman and the narrator look at the mouth of the tunnel but there is no spectre. This does not reassure the Signalman who is desperate to know what it means. He is sure 'some dreadful calamity will happen' (p. 115) and knows he has to do something, but does not know what. The fact he can see how unbelievable it all sounds makes him sound more convincing himself. We feel we have to agree with the narrator's verdict that the Signalman is suffering 'the mental torture of a conscientious man' (p. 115) and that he is not deranged or making it up.

> **CHECKPOINT 40**
>
> How does the Signalman know the difference between the real bell ring and the ghostly ringing?

> ### Responsibility
>
> An important word here is 'responsibility'. It is the Signalman's job to ensure the safety of the passengers on the Line. He believes that he is being warned of an imminent danger that could have terrible consequences if not prevented. But the spectre gives him no clue about what is going to happen: 'What is the danger? Where is the danger?' (p. 115). Dickens takes care to show the psychological effects of this on the Signalman. He is 'oppressed by an unintelligible responsibility involving life' (p. 115). There is more on **Responsibility** in the **Themes**.

CHECK THE NET

You can learn about life in Dickensian London and about other of Dickens' characters through an interactive game on the BBC website. Go to **www.bbc.co.uk** and type 'dickens game' into the search engine.

The narrator does not know what to do and, although he offers to stay through the night, leaves with a promise to return the next evening. We too leave the Signalman with the narrator and share the narrator's concern about what he should do. His discussion of the different options clarifies the situation and shows us that there is not an easy or obvious answer.

The next evening the narrator arrives near the cutting before it is time to return, but in looking down sees 'the appearance of a man, with his left sleeve across his eyes, passionately waving his right arm' (p. 117). This appears to be the spectre the Signalman had described so clearly, and it is as shocking to us as it is to our narrator.

However, no sooner are we surprised by this disturbing sight than we are told that the narrator has realised that it is a real person waving; indeed there are other people in the cutting. There is also a new object: 'a little low hut … no bigger than a bed' (p. 117). Our fears rise as we accompany the narrator into the cutting to find that the Signalman was killed that morning. The structure we saw from the top is a covering for the Signalman's body – the cutting that was so like a grave at the beginning of the story has got its coffin.

We are told that the Signalman was struck by a train even though the train driver was shouting at him to get out of the way. The train driver demonstrates his actions and call and we realise that they are the familiar words of the spectre. The third terrible event the Signalman was warned of was his own death.

But, in a final twist we learn that the last words the train driver used – 'For God's sake, clear the way!' (p. 114) – were never actually uttered by the spectre. Instead they were merely imagined by the narrator when the Signalman demonstrated how the spectre had waved at him. This 'coincidence' (p. 118) adds a further note of mystery at the end. Could it suggest that the spectre has somehow communicated to the narrator too?

CHECK THE FILM
Director Laurence Gordon Clarke directed the short film of 'The Signalman' for the BBC in 1976. It was re-released in 2002 by the British Film Institute. The film captures the atmosphere and tone of the story perfectly, but watch it carefully to see how the storyline has been changed.

Fate or free will?

This story raises some interesting questions:

- Was the Signalman's death his fate or was he driven to his death by the visions he saw?

- Should the narrator have taken action to prevent the Signalman's death?

- Are events already decided for us or do we have a say in the paths our lives take?

When you consider Dickens' belief in the value of education and his work as a social reformer, you might conclude he did not believe in the idea of pre-destined fate. When we add our knowledge of *A Christmas Carol* and 'The Poor Relation's Story' this conclusion seems even stronger.

Now take a break!

WHO SAYS '...?

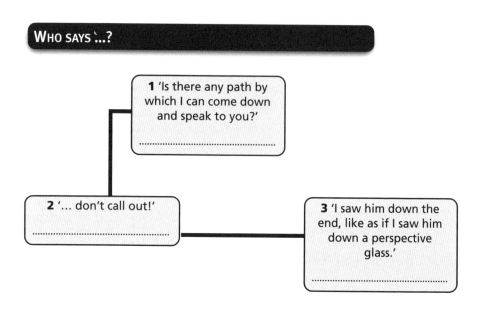

1 'Is there any path by which I can come down and speak to you?'

....

2 '... don't call out!'

....

3 'I saw him down the end, like as if I saw him down a perspective glass.'

....

ABOUT WHOM?

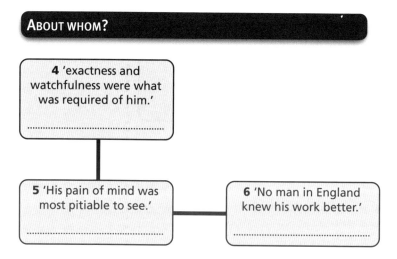

4 'exactness and watchfulness were what was required of him.'

....

5 'His pain of mind was most pitiable to see.'

....

6 'No man in England knew his work better.'

....

Check your answers on p. 119.

PART THREE

COMMENTARY

THEMES

RESPONSIBILITY

A key theme in these stories is responsibility. Dickens felt that every individual had a responsibility for those around him or her, and he exemplifies this belief in all three of these stories. Dickens' view of social responsibility was informed by his understanding of Christian teachings. He rejected rigid interpretations of the Bible in favour of more liberal readings that focused on the New Testament. Scrooge, in *A Christmas Carol*, articulates Dickens' contempt for Sabbatarianism, the movement that held Sunday as a sacred day where all activities had to be related to worship. Most people attended a church service and these stories reflect a general sense of 'Christian morality' where the individual is instructed to love and look after those less fortunate than him or herself. However, it must be remembered that attitudes to religion were changing during this time. Darwin's theory of evolution, *The Origin of Species*, was published for the first time in 1859, although he was discussing his ideas as early as 1853. The conflict between Darwin's ideas and more traditional ones, sparked debate about religion and human existence throughout society.

Scrooge learns to take responsibility for the poor, and in doing so redeems himself. Dickens had very little faith in, or respect for, political or church movements to counter poverty. He saw the New Poor Law as harsh and unfeeling and he felt the church schools set up to help children were too concerned with preaching rather than helping children out of poverty. When supporting the Ragged School movement he was keen to ensure they should teach children essential life skills such as reading and writing rather than to recite chunks of the Bible. Scrooge shows us the difference a wealthy individual can make, but Dickens also shows us Fezziwig's small contribution can make a significant difference to the lives of individuals.

 DID YOU KNOW?

Darwin's *The Origin of Species* describes the process by which all creatures have gradually evolved over millions of years from minute organisms to become the animals and plants we know today. This theory is in direct opposition to traditional Christian teaching, which holds that God created all living things exactly as they are now, over the course of six days at the beginning of time.

 **EXAMINER'S SECRET**

It is a good idea to use themes to compare stories – look at which themes come up and how they are dealt with.

DID YOU KNOW?

Dickens' preference for the New Testament was shown in his Will where he instructed his children to 'guide themselves by the teaching of the New Testament in its broad spirit, and to put no faith in any man's narrow construction of its letter here and there.'

DID YOU KNOW?

When Dickens joined his family in London he was surprised and upset not to be sent to school. He later said, 'what would I have given, if I had had anything to give, to have been sent back to any other school, to have been taught anything, anywhere!'

In 'The Poor Relation's Story' the emphasis is slightly different. Focusing on Michael, it shows that an individual can fall into hard times through lack of self-knowledge and drive. Michael's retreat into his 'Castle' shows him failing to take responsibility for his situation, and we know his life is not going to change for the better. However, Michael's narrative also throws light on the individuals involved in his downfall; John, for one, took advantage of him rather than helping him when he needed it.

'The Signalman' also shows the consequences of responsibility not being taken. The Signalman tells his story to the narrator who, rather than taking action, just thinks about what to do. If he had stayed with the Signalman, or taken action of some sort his death might have been avoided. Dickens makes us think about taking the harder route rather than letting life happen to us.

EDUCATION

The value of education is emphasised both in 'The Signalman' and *A Christmas Carol*. The Signalman very clearly feels that he is stuck in his job at the bottom of the grave-like cutting because he did not apply himself to his studies and was sent down from university (expelled). He is trying to make up for his lost education by teaching himself but we get the impression that the more he learns the more he realises his life might have been better as an adult if he had not 'run wild' (p. 108) as a young man.

The two children presented by the Ghost of Christmas Present are horrific in their appearance and serve to illustrate Dickens' belief in the power of and need for education. We are told to 'beware' Ignorance for he is 'Doom' (Stave Three, p. 73). The chilling language shows us how seriously Dickens takes the issue of education – he does not shy away from presenting the most graphic effects of ignorance and deprivation – and makes us think about the role of education in fighting poverty.

THE SUPERNATURAL

The supernatural is a theme that has interested authors through the ages. It refers to events or beings that are beyond human or scientific explanation, such as ghosts or seeing into the future.

The number of people who died every year in the Victorian era was much higher than it is today due to poverty and poorer standards of healthcare. Losing friends and family was a regular occurance and people thought a lot about what happened to the spirits of their loved ones after they had died. Dickens, like many Victorian authors, enjoyed working in the genre as it was popular and allowed stories to go beyond normal human experience.

Supernatural stories are often set in ordinary locations with ordinary characters. Having a convincing setting that the reader can relate to means that they are more likely to accept the event as supernatural. It also makes the supernatural seem even stranger by contrasting it with normal events. The reader has got to 'willingly suspend disbelief' to accept the event as supernatural rather than trying to provide a common-sense explanation. Therefore we have to be convinced that the Signalman is an educated and stable character to believe his visions of the spectre and that the ringing of the bell he hears is a supernatural occurrence rather then the product of his troubled mind. Likewise, it is important that we know that Scrooge's partner Marley is definitely dead so that there can be no other explanation for his reappearance than it is his ghost haunting Scrooge.

Although the Victorians had a solid tradition of ghost stories, perhaps the rising debate about the truth of the Bible and Christian theology at this time also helped to make this genre a popular one. If there is a purely scientific explanation for life, then the supernatural cannot exist.

THE POWER OF THE IMAGINATION

Dickens firmly believed in the power of the imagination and we see it as a means of liberation for both Michael and the young Scrooge.

Michael's 'Castle' is a place of retreat, especially during Christmas and New Year, where he can live a fantasy life and forget about his real life. Every day for him is essentially a day he must get through; he has nothing to look forward to except his own death. The 'Castle' allows him to imagine all is well, if not perfect, and this makes us realise the power of the imagination to free a person from reality.

 CHECK THE NET
You can find out about the Victorian craze for spiritualism – a belief that the spirits of the dead can be contacted through a medium – on the following website: **www.victorianweb.org**. Click on 'Religion' and then on 'Spiritualism'.

DID YOU KNOW?
Dickens took refuge in books and stories when he was in London without schooling or a role in the family. He also spend much time walking around London, learning all about it, which must be one of the reasons he writes about so much of it in so much detail in his books.

The young Scrooge also finds comfort in the power of the imagination. Left at school over Christmas he resorts to reading stories of fantastical characters such as Ali Baba and Robinson Crusoe. The older Scrooge's obvious delight at seeing these characters again demonstrates how vibrant and powerful they must have been to the boy and how much they must have helped him get through his loneliness.

ISOLATION

The need for companionship and company is demonstrated in all three of these stories. Left to himself as a boy, Scrooge found companionship in stories, but as an adult it led him to focus on money at the expense of personal relationships. The difference in the early Scrooge and the redeemed Scrooge is considerable, and we see that it is not just due to his helping the poor; it is as a result of his re-joining society. Becoming a second father to Tiny Tim means Scrooge gets some of the love and support he has been missing or refusing.

Michael relies on Little Frank – he says they understand each other, and we see his sense of desperation at the idea of the boy being sent away to school. He does not have anyone else; he is obviously only invited to John's house at Christmas, and Little Frank's mother does not approve of him. He fills his 'Castle' with people and children, showing his need for human company. The title of the story sums him up perfectly; because he is without love or money he truly is 'The Poor Relation'.

The Signalman's concerns are made harder to bear due to his lack of human company. It takes him time to tell the narrator his story, and he is obviously worried about being regarded as unwell. Part of this is the fact he spends his time in the signal box, away from society.

POVERTY

The theme of poverty is prevalent in Dickens' work, especially those novels and stories set in cities, such as *A Christmas Carol* and 'The Poor Relation's Story'. It is interesting that 'The Signalman' does not deal with this issue, perhaps suggesting that Dickens felt poverty and its effects were not such an issue in the countryside.

The poverty described in *A Christmas Carol* and 'The Poor Relation's Story' is not the harsh, striking poverty as seen in *Oliver Twist*; the Cratchits have a Christmas goose and Michael has a room. However, these are people living on the edge: Bob Cratchit and Michael can only just afford the lives they lead. Mrs Cratchit's ribbons might be a luxury but they are also a symbol of her desperation to make her dress look new and respectable again. The Cratchits might be full at the end of their meal, but we have to wonder if this is because they don't have enough to eat the rest of the year.

STRUCTURE

THE STRUCTURE OF A NOVELLA

A Christmas Carol follows the typical structure of a novella. The scene is set and characters are established very quickly. It is made clear to us that Marley is indeed dead, but the excessive focus on him makes us realise that he will be significant. This becomes true when he becomes the **precipitating incident** that sets the story in motion. The text then follows the standard structure for a novella with each ghost developing the action, or creating **rising action**. Scrooge's repentance adds to this but he faces a **reversal** when he will not look at the face of the dead man in the bed. This leads to the **climax** of his gravestone; the moment of highest impact and tension and the one that causes the permanent change in Scrooge. Stave Five follows the path of **falling action** as we see how Scrooge has in fact changed, leading to the **resolution** where Tiny Tim has not died.

Each section of *A Christmas Carol* is called a Stave instead of a Chapter. A stave is the five lines that music is written on. This is Dickens' way of playing with the structure and reminding us this is a Christmas story, rather like the carols sung at Christmas time – it contains a message of new life and possibilities. Just as there are five lines in the musical stave, so there are five movements to his story. He also wrote this story to be read aloud, much as carols are sung aloud.

EXAMINER'S SECRET

Knowledge and use of social, cultural and historical detail in your writing will get you a higher grade.

EXAMINER'S SECRET

Don't be afraid to use terms such as 'structure'. Used properly they will allow you to show you understand how the text works.

This diagram shows the structure of a novella, as demonstrated in *A Christmas Carol*:

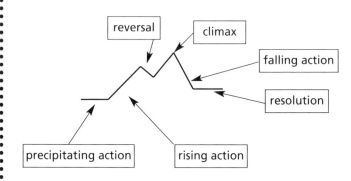

THE STRUCTURE OF A SHORT STORY

'The Poor Relation's Story' and 'The Signalman' are written according to standard structures of short stories. This structure is like that of the novella but without the **reversal**:

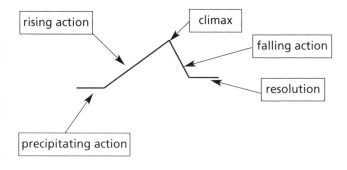

The structure of 'The Poor Relation's Story':

1. **Precipitating incident**: Michael is asked to tell a story.
2. **Rising action**: He rejects the family's notions of him and tells of his 'real life'.
3. **Climax**: He says he lives in a Castle.
4. **Resolution**: He admits his 'Castle' is in the air.

The structure of 'The Signalman':

1. **Precipitating incident**: The narrator sees the Signalman and goes to talk to him. He unwittingly calls out using the same words as the spectre has used.
2. **Rising action**: The Signalman has seen a spectre before two fatal accidents.
3. **Climax**: The Signalman is killed. We find out the driver warned him using the same wave and words as the spectre.
4. **Resolution**: The narrator realises the story has come full circle; the words and actions were the same and the Signalman's death appeared to be inevitable.

With both 'The Poor Relation's Story' and 'The Signalman' the action develops towards the climax throughout. There is no **subplot** or **deviation** and, once the climax is reached, the story is wrapped up or resolved very quickly.

CHARACTERS

A CHRISTMAS CAROL

EBENEZER SCROOGE

One of Dickens' most famous characters, the word 'Scrooge' has become part of the English language to describe anyone mean or miserly or showing disapproval at others enjoying themselves.

At the beginning of the novella, Scrooge is described with wonderful clarity, 'a tight-fisted hand at the grindstone', 'a squeezing, wrenching, grasping, scraping, clutching, covetous old sinner!' (Stave One, p. 12). The adjectives and **similes** mount up to create an overwhelming impression of this mean and fierce old man

Begins:
Mean
Cold-hearted
Callous
Ends:
Loving
Generous
Happy

whose bitterness even influences the weather. He has no friends, no-one ever asks how he is; and, to underline his miserable nature, we are told that he prefers it this way.

Although this hard misanthropist revels in his own harsh opinions at the start of the novella – he has 'an improved opinion of himself' (Stave One, p. 18) after his exchange with the Charity Collectors – Scrooge reveals his humanity when he understands Tiny Tim might die due to his actions and opinions. At this point he becomes 'overcome with penitence and grief' (Stave Three, p. 63). This change is made permanent by the horrors Scrooge suffers in Stave Four – he is literally faced with his own death.

In the final Stave we see a joyous, happy man, completely transformed from the one we met at the beginning of the novella. He is happy to be alive, and in spreading this happiness creates yet more. His altered behaviour – 'rubbing his hands and splitting with a laugh' (Stave Five, p. 91) – combined with his generous actions to those around him, persuade us that he is a changed man.

Hard working
Family man
Caring
Passive

BOB CRATCHIT

Bob is a passive, kind-hearted man who cannot object to the way he is treated by Scrooge. Representative of the lower classes, he has to accept the poor wages and working conditions because he has a family to support and a badly-paid job is better than no job. He is little more than a caricature with his long 'white comforter dangling below his waist' instead of a coat (Stave One, p. 19). His good nature is his dominant characteristic, as seen when he toasts Scrooge as 'the Founder of the Feast' (Stave Three, p. 63).

TINY TIM

Tiny Tim is one of Dickens' most famous characters, although one that causes controversy today. A stock character of Victorian literature, the innocent disabled child often dies or is saved through no fault or action of their own. This character has caused offence and argument today, especially amongst readers who see this character as being insulting to disabled people. Today disabled people are not considered passive victims. Whatever the modern view however, it is important to understand the function Tiny Tim plays in the novella; he is the innocent vehicle for Scrooge's redemption.

Disabled
Loving
Vulnerable

FRED

Fred is the antithesis of Scrooge. Jovial and good-natured he married for love without thinking about money and is not merely concerned with profit (Stave One, p. 14). He acts as a **foil** to the hardened Scrooge and provides a means of support and redemption once he is reformed. A supporting character, Fred is defined by his good humour and laughter whilst articulating many of Dickens' beliefs about Christmas. To Fred (and Dickens) it is 'a good time; a kind, forgiving, charitable, pleasant time … when men and women seem by one consent to open their shut-up hearts freely, and to think of people below them as if they really were fellow-passengers to the grave, and not another race of creatures bound on other journeys' (Stave One, p. 15).

Good natured
Jovial
Generous

MARLEY'S GHOST

Weighed down with chains and baggage **symbolising** the concerns he had in life, Marley's Ghost appears as a warning to Scrooge on the anniversary of Marley's death. His desperation to now help the poor and needy, awakens Scrooge to the seriousness of his own situation. He has echoes of Hamlet's father's ghost with his wanderings and restlessness and the 'incessant torture of remorse' he suffers (Stave One, p. 26).

THE GHOSTS OF CHRISTMAS PAST, PRESENT AND YET TO COME

These Ghosts act as **metaphors** for Scrooge's life. They represent what he has been, what he is and what he is going to be if he doesn't change. Although the first two Ghosts make Scrooge face up to the consequences of his actions they are jovial and sympathetic. The final Ghost is far harsher, refusing to provide comfort or support; Scrooge has to draw his own conclusions and change his life himself.

Desperate
In agony
Regretful

**Represents lost
innocence
Gentle
Mild
Insistent**

**Jovial
Gigantic
Stern**

**Bleak
Chilling
Merciless**

The Ghost of Christmas Past personifies what Scrooge has been, His appearance, 'like a child; yet not so like a child as like an old man' (Stave Two, p. 33), reminds us that Scrooge's childhood is long gone. The white tunic represents the innocence that should be part of childhood, and it is decorated with summer flowers, a reminder that this Spirit represents Scrooge's 'summer' years. Its cap, which Scrooge pushes down at the end of the Stave, represents the negative emotions, actions and ideas Scrooge adopted during his later years, and which hide and suppress his true nature.

The Ghost of Christmas Present **personifies** generosity; both spiritual and material. He wears a large green robe trimmed with white fur, reminding us there is still innocence in the world. Surrounded by plenty and sitting on a throne of food, this Ghost reminds us there is enough to go round in the world, contradicting the Malthusian economic Dickens so hated (see **Setting and background**). However, despite this Ghost's appearance of compassion and plenty, it conceals the harsh realities of Victorian life in the shape of the children Ignorance and Want.

The Ghost of Christmas Yet to Come personifies death which is inevitable for all humans (as mentioned by Fred in Stave One). It is a terrifying figure, 'shrouded in a deep black garment, which concealed its head, its face, its form' (Stave Four, p. 74). We are unable to distinguish its features, reminding us that the exact details are unknown until it strikes. Just as time will not stop for anyone, so the Ghost will not wait for Scrooge; it just leads him from scene to scene, pointing out what he must see.

'THE POOR RELATION'S STORY'

MICHAEL

Michael represents those people for whom life has not gone to plan. He has always been dominated by others, and his passivity has led to the unhappy situation he is now in where he has to retreat to an imaginary world to escape the monotony of life. We see sparks of life in him when he speaks of Little Frank and the world of his 'Castle', but these only serve to highlight the waste of a human life. His life consists of making the time go past; he is just waiting for his death. Although he demonstrates the power of the imagination, he also raises the issue of equality and examines how society and individuals treat those not as strong as the majority.

Weak
Trampled-on
Clever
Imaginative

UNCLE CHILL

Uncle Chill is a typical Dickensian character; he exists only to represent the harshness of the world and the unfeeling nature of many in society at the time. He can be summarised by his name; this **characternym** tells us all we need to know about his personality. His domestic, Betsy Snap, has a similar role.

Cold
Cruel
Uncaring

'THE SIGNALMAN'

Neither the narrator or the Signalman are fully drawn characters; the importance of this story lies in the events.

THE NARRATOR

The narrator is an anonymous character in 'The Signalman'; it is only from reading the whole 'Mugby Junction' sequence of short stories that we learn his name. His anonymity in 'The Signalman' makes him representative of all travellers or people looking for answers. Dickens also uses him to show what perils result from failing to act to help another in distress (see **Theme** on **Responsibility**).

Interested in others
Inquisitive
Sympathetic
Does not act when he could do

Diligent
Dutiful
Troubled
Wasted his
education

THE SIGNALMAN

The Signalman represents the individual whose choices in life have led to a dead-end; the signal-box at the bottom of the cutting represents this. We are told he didn't make the most of his educational opportunities, as 'he had run wild, misused his opportunities, gone down, and never risen again' (p. 108). This links to Dickens' belief in the power of education, but also serves to make us more likely to believe his story of the spectre; an educated and intelligent man seems less likely to make up such an event or have such a fantasy.

The Signalman's appearance reflects the stress that he has been under and also the dark, gloomy place that he works: 'he was a dark, sallow man, with a dark beard and rather heavy eyebrows' (p. 106). He feels the responsibility of his job (see **Theme** on **Responsibility**) and takes it very seriously. He is diligent and methodical in all his tasks, showing that he is rational and not deluded.

LANGUAGE AND STYLE

Students make common errors when starting to talk or write about the writer's use of language. It is probably one of the more difficult aspects of literature. In this section you will be given some information about the language used by Charles Dickens and some pointers as to how to go about discussing it.

Dickens is famous for his use of language to describe people, places and features of landscape.

CHARACTERS

A favourite technique Dickens uses to create character is through their names; these often give the reader an idea of their character. This is known as a **characternym**. In these stories we find:

- Ebenezer Scrooge – gnarled and mean, refuses to look beyond money.
- The Cratchits – poor, scratching out a living and only surviving through mutual support, acting as a crutch for each other.
- Uncle Chill – cold, harsh and unforgiving.

EXAMINER'S
SECRET
Collect adjectives and quotations about each character to help you revise.

Dickens also makes good use of imagery to present his characters and help explain their personalities. Appearance is often linked to personality, and we are given a clear indication about Scrooge's likely behaviour from his appearance. He is described using lists of adjectives and many **similes**; this helps us to get a clear image of what he looks like as well as his personality:

'The cold within him froze his old features, nipped his pointed nose, shrivelled his cheek, stiffened his gait; made his eyes red, his thin lips blue; and spoke out shrewdly in his grating voice.'
(Stave One, p. 12)

The extended image of the cold freezing Scrooge up is made more effective by the adjectives that help us picture exactly what his nose, lips and voice are like. The fact his nose is 'pointed' emphasises his sharp and unforgiving nature.

Other characters also described by this use of language:

- The Ghost of Christmas Past has a long and complicated description, reflecting its complicated nature; the past is a fact yet memory is not always clear or reliable. Therefore we are given descriptions such as, 'like a child; yet not so like a child as like an old man' and, 'its hair … was white, as if with age; and yet the face had not a wrinkle in it' (Stave Two, p. 33). These seemingly contradictory statements remind us that Scrooge's childhood was a long time ago, and the child this Ghost represents is in the past. This gives us an old child.

- Betsy Snap is described using a similar technique; we are told she is 'a withered, hard-favoured, yellow old woman' (p. 119) and this unpleasant description combines with her name to create a negative image.

Dickens also focuses on actions and behaviour to help bring his characters to life:

- Fred is always described in positive terms, often laughing, 'holding his sides, rolling his head, and twisting his face into the most extravagant contortions' (Stave Three, p. 67), and always

EXAMINER'S SECRET

Try to work out what the 'function' of each character is: why are they included in the story?

EXAMINER'S SECRET

Draw or cut out pictures to represent each character and help you remember them. Many people find it easier to remember pictures or images, even if they are abstract.

good-humoured, to contrast with Scrooge. This detailed description of Fred's laughter helps us to visualise exactly how he is behaving.

- The Signalman's mysterious and nervous behaviour tells us very quickly that something is wrong, 'He directed a most curious look towards the red light near the tunnel's mouth, and looked all about it, as if something were missing from it, and then looked at me' (p. 107). Dickens describes precisely where and how the Signalman directs his gaze, allowing us to visualise this action exactly. The fact that he is so intent on looking about him shows his nervousness.

When writing about character it is essential to pick out the key quotations that summarise that character and your ideas about him or her. It is a good idea to explain what this quotation shows or suggests:

Scrooge is described as being 'solitary as an oyster' (Stave One, p. 12). This simile suggests he is shut up, tightly closed and will not be prised open except by force. However, oysters often contain pearls, so this simile also suggests there might be good buried deep inside him, underneath the hard, brittle shell.

When the narrator is the central **protagonist** it is harder to analyse them as they will not be described in so much detail. Therefore we have to look at what they decide to tell us and how they tell us this.

Michael's small comments about John look very complimentary on the surface – he calls him 'our esteemed host', 'my friend and partner' (pp. 114, 124). However, when we add this to our knowledge of Michael's situation we realise the John isn't the wonderful person this suggests. After taking over Michael's business John pays him a quarterly allowance but this cannot be as generous as implied because Michael is living in a room he cannot afford to heat and has to spend carefully. When it is revealed that the 'Castle' is imaginary we immediately realise that John's fair and supportive behaviour as 'friend and partner' must belong to that imaginary world and that his actual behaviour is probably quite different. This

EXAMINER'S SECRET
Don't just identify a *simile* or *metaphor*: explain what it does and why it has been used.

shows us that Michael is far sharper and cleverer than his lifestyle would suggest. He criticises John implicitly, which is far more powerful than just explaining that he feels hard done by.

SETTING THE SCENE AND CREATING THE ATMOSPHERE

Dickens creates richly descriptive scenes through his use of adjectives and imagery.

The railway cutting in 'The Signalman' is described as a 'great dungeon' from where you can see 'the gloomier entrance to a black tunnel, in whose massive architecture there was a barbarous, depressing, and forbidding air' (p. 106). The image of a dungeon is easy to visualise and the adjectives describing the air of the tunnel combine to create an overwhelming sense of despair.

He uses similar techniques when describing the graveyard where Scrooge's future gravestone lies (if he does not change his ways). 'Walled in by houses; overrun by grass and weeds, the growth of vegetation's death, not life; choked up with too much burying; fat with repleted appetite' (Stave Four, p. 87). The exact description allows the reader to picture what this space looks like, but then goes on to touch on aspects of life and death that are not normally discussed – the death of these people has given life to these weeds. The benefit the weeds gain from the dead Scrooge reminds us of the benefit the thieves gained from stealing from him. Neither Scrooge's body nor his wealth can be described as doing good after his death as they feed the grossly abundant, unwanted aspects of society.

The joy of Fezziwig's party contrasts starkly with these scenes due to the overwhelming sense of fun and plenty provided. 'There were more dances, and there were forfeits, and more dances, and there was cake, and there was negus, and there was a great piece of Cold Roast, and there was a great piece of Cold Boiled, and there were mincepies, and plenty of beer' (Stave Two, p. 42). This **compound sentence** builds up the sense of plenty by adding more and more in a list, implying that the narrator can only just keep up with all there is to see and do. Using the connective 'and' rather than just listing with commas helps to make it overwhelming.

EXAMINER'S SECRET
Read the information on the exam paper carefully and highlight your task.

EXAMINER'S SECRET
Use highlighters to cross-reference similar techniques or ideas in different texts.

EXAMINER'S SECRET

When you open your exam paper make sure you read all the questions and don't just start the first one you see: it might not be the best one!

Remember the following points about any text you read:

- The writer started off with a blank page.

- Every word has been deliberately chosen to create a world that is not real. (You could say that the text is a construct.)

- One form of words may be far more effective than another in getting across a particular idea or feeling.

- The writer sets out to do something – not simply to fill the page – you have to identify what this aim was.

- You should discuss whether the writer has been effective, e.g., is a frightening passage actually frightening?

- Finally, try to develop an appreciation for style. This can only be done by reading the work of different writers. You need to have your own opinion as to how good Dickens is at expressing ideas and emotions and how he does it.

Now take a break!

PART FOUR

RESOURCES

HOW TO USE QUOTATIONS

One of the secrets of success in writing essays is the way you use quotations. There are five basic principles:

1 Put inverted commas at the beginning and end of the quotation.

2 Write the quotation exactly as it appears in the original.

3 Do not use a quotation that repeats what you have just written.

4 Use the quotation so that it fits into your sentence.

5 Keep the quotation as short as possible.

Quotations should be used to develop the line of thought in your essays. Your comment should not duplicate what is in your quotation. For example:

Scrooge is tight-fisted and works everyone to the grindstone: 'Oh! But he was a tight-fisted hand at the grindstone' (Stave One, p. 12).

It is much more effective to write:

The narrator emphasises how mean and strict Scrooge is, especially focusing on the way he keeps everyone working: 'Oh! But he was a tight-fisted hand at the grindstone' (Stave One, p. 12).

The most sophisticated way of using the writer's words is to embed them into your sentence:

The 'tight-fisted' (Stave One, p. 12) **Scrooge pushes everyone to the limit, working them to the** 'grindstone' (Stave One, p. 12). **This emphasises Scrooge's harsh and ungenerous nature; he is closed up and like stone, wearing everyone down.**

When you use quotations in this way, you are demonstrating the

EXAMINER'S SECRET

Short and concise quotations are the best ones.

EXAMINER'S SECRET

Even if you are allowed to take your text into the exam room, try to learn a key quotation for each main character – this only needs to be one word. It will help you learn the story and mean you don't have to spend so much time looking for the quotation you know is there somewhere!

EXAMINER'S SECRET

The best answers embed the quotations into their answers.

EXAMINER'S SECRET

If you plan your answer before you start writing it you will end up with a more focused and logical essay.

ability to use text as evidence to support your ideas – not simply including words from the original to prove you have read it.

Coursework Essay

Set aside an hour or so at the start of your work to plan what you have to do.

- List all the points you feel are needed to cover the task. Collect page references of information and quotations that will support what you have to say. A helpful tool is the highlighter pen: this saves painstaking copying and enables you to target precisely what you want to use.

- Focus on what you consider to be the main points of the essay. Try to sum up your argument in a single sentence, which could be the closing sentence of your essay. Depending on the essay title, it could be a statement about character: The 'as good as gold' (Stave Three, p. 58) Tiny Tim provides a refreshing contrast to the misanthropic Scrooge and shows us that it is possible to be positive despite adversity; an opinion about setting: The location of the Signalman's box, at the bottom of the dark and gloomy cutting, sets the tone for the supernatural story; it is as if we enter another world as we descend to it with the narrator; or a judgement on a theme: Michael's retreat to his 'Castle' celebrates the power of the imagination whilst highlighting social injustice.

- Make a short essay plan. Use the first paragraph to introduce the argument you wish to make. In the following paragraphs develop this argument with details, examples and other possible points of view. Sum up your argument in the last paragraph. Check you have answered the question.

- Write the essay, remembering to keep returning to the central point you are making.

- On completion, go back over what you have written to eliminate careless errors and improve expression. Read it aloud to yourself, or, if you are feeling more confident, to a relative or friend.

If you can, try to type your essay, using a word processor. This will allow you to correct and improve your writing without spoiling its appearance.

SITTING THE EXAMINATION

Examination papers are carefully designed to give you the opportunity to do your best. Follow these handy hints for exam success:

BEFORE YOU START

- Make sure you know the subject of the examination so that you are properly prepared and equipped.

- You need to be comfortable and free from distractions. Inform the invigilator if anything is off-putting, e.g., a shaky desk.

- Read the instructions, or rubric, on the front of the examination paper. You should know by now what you have to do, but check to reassure yourself.

- Observe the time allocation – and follow it carefully. If they recommend 60 minutes for Question 1 and 30 minutes for Question 2, it is because Question 1 carries twice as many marks.

- Consider the mark allocation. You should write a longer response for 4 marks than for 2 marks.

WRITING YOUR RESPONSES

- Use the questions to structure your response, e.g., question: 'Do you believe in Scrooge's transformation? Compare the way he is presented before the Ghosts visit him with the way he is presented at the end of the novella.' The first part of your answer will analyse the description of Scrooge in Stave One; the second part will look at the ending of the novella; the third part will be comparison of his behaviour and how it is presented, leading to your conclusion.

- Write a brief draft outline of your response.

EXAMINER'S SECRET

An analysis of students' exam scripts showed higher grade answers had plans. This either means plans lead to higher grade answers or higher grade students write plans. Whichever it is it's a good reason for a plan!

EXAMINER'S SECRET

If you are allowed to take your text into the examination room, check what notes you are permitted to have made in it.

EXAMINER'S SECRET

It doesn't matter what other people do in their exam time: you are the one who counts once you have entered the exam hall.

EXAMINER'S SECRET

The more you prepare the better your answer will be.

- A typical 30-minute examination essay is probably between 400 and 600 words in length.

- Keep your writing legible and easy to read, using paragraphs to show the structure of your answers.

- Spend a couple of minutes afterwards quickly checking for obvious errors.

WHEN YOU HAVE FINISHED

- Don't be downhearted – if you found the examination difficult, it is probably because you really worked at the questions. Let's face it, they are not meant to be easy!

EXAMINER'S SECRET

Don't just retell the story. You need to explain how and why it does or doesn't work.

- Don't pay too much attention to what your friends have to say about the paper. Everyone's experience is different and no two people ever give the same answers.

IMPROVE YOUR GRADE

The first stage in improving your grade is to engage with the text and ask yourself these questions:

- Why does this text exist? What message is the writer trying to convey?
- What techniques have been used to convey this message?
- Does it work? Was the writer successful? Is it still relevant today?

EXAMINER'S SECRET

Don't forget your social, cultural, historical and literary context.

WHY DOES THIS TEXT EXIST? WHAT MESSAGE IS THE WRITER TRYING TO CONVEY?

It takes months, even years to write books (think how long your last coursework essay took to write and work out how much longer a book is!). Each book is written for a purpose. This purpose might be to entertain, but often it is to convey a message the author feels strongly about.

These stories are all 'Christmas Stories', but they were written to be read at Christmas as much as being about Christmas. Dickens' childhood experiences influenced much of *A Christmas Carol*. His ideas about social reform and humanity can be seen in 'The Poor Relation's Story' and the train crash in Kent influenced 'The Signalman'. However, his writing is more complex than merely having one theme or idea and you should look at the different events in each story and think about what he is trying to say. However, underpinning all of his writing is a desire to entertain.

WHAT TECHNIQUES HAVE BEEN USED TO CONVEY THIS MESSAGE?

This means you need to explore the way Dickens conveys, or puts across, his messages and ideas. Many students panic at this point and just re-tell the story: this is not what you are being asked to do and will not attract many marks. You need to use your knowledge of how the story works and show how a particular scene or character's behaviour persuades the reader to respond in a certain way. For example, Scrooge's treatment of his nephew, the Charity Collectors and Bob Cratchit makes us dislike him and reject his opinions.

DOES IT WORK? WAS THE WRITER SUCCESSFUL? IS IT STILL RELEVANT TODAY?

This is about evaluating what Dickens has done. You need to be clear about his aims and purposes in order to judge whether he achieved them or not. You will need to:

- Outline his aims and purposes.

- Explore how he goes about achieving them.

- Evaluate how successful he is.

For example, if you think Dickens set out to create believable characters, has he managed this? Do you think he intended us to feel some sympathy for Scrooge, and, if so, has he made us feel it?

Although you should avoid using the first person pronoun 'I' in the main body of your essay (i.e., 'I think', 'I feel'), the examiner is looking for your ideas and responses to a text. If you can see how the text might link to an event or situation today then put it in and

EXAMINER'S SECRET

Take note of the time allocated for each answer and stick to it. Make sure you can see the clock in the examination room.

EXAMINER'S SECRET

If you can see a modern parallel to a character or theme in the book mention it, but don't lose your focus on the book you're being tested on.

EXAMINER'S SECRET

Make sure you keep your focus on the question you have been set. A good way to do this is to use the terms or language of the question at the end of every paragraph. This will ensure you bring your ideas back to answering the question.

EXAMINER'S SECRET

Don't get confused between the author and the narrator. Sometimes Dickens uses a character to narrate a story, but sometimes he invents an unseen narrator. The narrator might voice his ideas, but is not necessarily Dickens himself.

explain it. The conclusion is a really good place for a personal response, but remember: you must have evidence for your opinions – they will mean nothing without it.

WRITING ABOUT LANGUAGE AND STYLE

A characteristic that often marks high-level answers is the willingness to write about language and style. Don't be scared about this – if you get an impression of the setting through the language, or you can use an image to make a link with another part of the text, then explain it.

- Dickens often uses **imagery** to create impressions in the reader's mind. For example, when the narrator first observes the railway cutting in which the Signalman works he likens it to a grave or hell:

  So little sunlight ever found its way to this spot, that it had an earthy, deadly smell; and so much cold wind rushed through it, that it struck chill to me, as if I had left the natural world. (p. 106)

The lack of sunlight, which represents life, and the concept of leaving the natural world creates a chilling and sinister atmosphere of fear and dread.

- Dickens includes the idea of God watching Scrooge's actions with 'the gruff old bell … always peeping slily down at Scrooge' (Stave One, p. 18).

The fact this is a church bell and part of a clock reminds us of the omniscient God who can see all we do. The clock represents time passing, or in Scrooge's case, time running out.

Key **images** and **symbols** such as the villain dressed in black and the hero in white have been used by writers for years (think about Darth Vader and Luke Skywalker in *Star Wars*!). The more books you read or films you watch, the more ideas about symbols you will pick up. Symbols might have different meanings for different readers or in different contexts, but as long as you explain the ideas you draw from a text and provide evidence your reading will be valid.

● Dickens is an expert at creating character through description and **dialogue**. Fred's constant laughter and sparkling eyes make him attractive and indicate his personality: 'he was all in a glow; his face was ruddy and handsome; his eyes sparkled, and his breath smoked again' (Stave One, p. 14).

This creates a clear image of a healthy, happy man, and we immediately contrast him with Scrooge and his appearance: 'A frosty rime was on his head, and on his eyebrows, and his wiry chin' (Stave One, p. 12).

Scrooge's appearance is old and cold and dry; we are much more likely to side with Fred's ideas than Scrooge's.

● Characters are also given dialogue that helps to shape our response to them; Scrooge's 'Bah, Humbug' (Stave One, p. 14) is an expression of disbelief and rejection and has become as famous as Scrooge himself.

THE EXAMINER'S VIEWPOINT

There are key features of students' answers that can be categorised as basic, better and best:

Basic

Students often ignore the question and just write all they know about the text or a character. They forget to use quotations to support their ideas e.g., **'Uncle Chill is not very nice to Michael'**.

This sort of answer is either given by someone who doesn't really know the text they are being tested on, or someone who is so keen to write down all they know they don't look at the question.

Better

An answer in this category will see some attempt to engage with, and answer, the question. There will be some quotations but they will often be left to speak for themselves as the student will not have provided any analysis or explanation of them.

EXAMINER'S SECRET

Check to see if you are allowed to take a bottle of still water into the examination room. If you are it will help you keep your concentration during the exam (but don't drink so much that you waste time going to the toilet!)

EXAMINER'S SECRET

Find out the assessment objectives or criteria for your exam or coursework before you start revising.

This sort of answer is often given by someone who knows what they have to do but finds it difficult to provide specific detail about what is happening in the text. They might think an idea is obvious and so not provide detail about it. They sometimes run in the trap of re-telling the story.

EXAMINER'S SECRET

Practice linking your answers to the information listed in the assessment objectives.

Best

An answer in this category will not provide a re-telling of the plot as the candidate will realise the examiner has read the book. They will engage with the question and plan carefully to address it throughout their response. This answer will have lots of short quotations, often integrated into the main body of the essay. These quotations will be directly addressed and explored, with specific words or features highlighted and their effects explained.

The conclusion will often include a fully explained personal response to the text.

In summary, you should:

- Consider why this text exists and the message it contains

- Provide specific and detailed analysis of the techniques that have been used

- Include your personal response

SAMPLE ESSAY PLAN

A typical essay question on *A Christmas Carol* is followed by a sample essay plan in note form. This does not present the only answer to the question, merely one answer. Do not be afraid to include your own ideas and leave out some of those in the sample! Remember that quotations are essential to prove and illustrate the points you make.

Why did Dickens write *A Christmas Carol*?

Look carefully at the question. The key word is 'why'. You need to consider the message of the text and any factors that might have contributed to its existence. This means you will need knowledge of Dickens' life and beliefs as well as a good knowledge of the story. You may find it useful to plan your writing in the following manner.

Part 1

- The message of the text is summarised by Marley's Ghost: 'Mankind was my business' (Stave One, p. 26).

- We are shown the need to think of others and not just focus on self-gain.

- Dickens' experiences of poverty and his belief in the power of education might have influenced him.

Part 2

- Scrooge is such an unpleasant character we reject him and his values.

- Other characters such as Fred and Bob Cratchit provide contrast and show alternative, happier, ways of living.

Part 3

- We follow Scrooge on his journey and believe what the Ghosts show him of his past, present and future because it fits his current character.

- The Ghost of Christmas Past starts to provide some reasons for Scrooge's behaviour. Although we do not forgive his actions we can start to understand how a terror of being poor led him to focus purely on money.

- It is ironic that Dickens could describe Scrooge in this way whilst also having a terror of being poor; he did not give up work when he was ill due to this.

Part 4

- The Ghost of Christmas Present reinforces the message of the Ghost of Christmas Past.

EXAMINER'S SECRET

Make sure you put a line through your plan to make it clear it is not part of the main essay. Don't cross it out as it might get you extra marks.

- Tiny Tim brings out Scrooge's compassionate side and we realise there is a chance he might change.

- The children, Ignorance and Want, are shocking illustrations of the poverty at the time and support Dickens' belief about the need for education.

Part 5

- The Ghost of Christmas Yet to Come provides disturbing but effective images of what will happen if Scrooge does not make mankind his business.

- Scrooge's reaction seems genuine and we believe he truly means to change.

Part 6

- The final Stave is a joyful one, showing the benefits for all if Dickens' message is taken to heart. Not only does Tiny Tim live, but Scrooge is reborn and also has a new life.

- We are left with a warm feeling at this happy ending and believe Scrooge's change of heart.

- The story will not leave us, but will 'haunt us pleasantly' (Preface) as Dickens hoped.

COMPARING STORIES

EXAMINER'S SECRET

If you are asked to compare two stories try to do so throughout your essay, not just in the conclusion.

If you are comparing stories you need to work out what is similar and what is different about each story, for example there are ghosts in *A Christmas Carol* and 'The Signalman' but not in 'The Poor Relation's Story'. This then leads to the question of why, and what this story does instead to raise issues about reality and fantasy. Is the 'Castle' of Michael's imagination very different to the supernatural events in the other two texts?

Make sure you plan your essay in terms of themes rather than story by story as this will allow you to compare the stories as you go, not just as an add-on at the end of your essay.

FURTHER QUESTIONS

Make a plan as shown above and attempt these questions.

1 How does Dickens present the poor and poverty in *A Christmas Carol* and 'The Poor Relation's Story'?

2 Explore Dickens' characterisation in at least two of his stories.

3 Dickens didn't just write to entertain. Analyse the message of one or more of his stories.

4 Dickens structures his stories very carefully. Analyse the structure of two of his short stories or novellas.

5 Can we ever believe in Scrooge's transformation?

6 'Whilst Dickens' main characters are full of life, his supporting characters are merely functional.' Do you agree? Why?

7 Explore the role of setting and atmosphere in Dickens' work.

8 What does Dickens have to say about industrialisation and the city?

9 What is the meaning of the Preface to *A Christmas Carol*?

10 Write about the way contemporary views of children are presented in *A Christmas Carol* and at least one other story of the period.

EXAMINER'S SECRET

Try making up and answering your own questions using the assessment objectives or mark scheme.

characternym a name given to a character which makes suggestions about that person's manner or appearance

cliché a phrase or expression that is so overused it has lost its meaning

climax the high point of a story, the moment of highest action and tension

compound sentence a sentence made up of one or more equal clauses (parts) joined by a connective (such as 'and')

construct an invention of the writer, crafted for a purpose

deviation to move away from what is currently happening or expected

dialogue a discussion or conversation, or simply the words spoken by a character

falling action a reduction of the tension in a story which allows events to slow down. This comes after a climax

first person narrative the narrator speaks as 'I' and normally takes part in the story

foil something or someone with opposite characteristics to the subject, used to balance them out and even to draw attention to their failings

image, imagery an image is a picture in words. Similes, metaphors, and personification are all types of imagery

irony/ironic saying or writing one thing when you mean, or want to imply, another; often used to show that the opposite is in fact true

juxtaposition to place two contrasting events or descriptions side by side for effect

metaphor a word or image which means one thing is used to represent another to show something interesting or different about it

novella a prose story shorter than a novel but longer than a short story. It has one main character and plot

omniscient narrator a narrator who can see everything and so can move the focus from character to character and scene to scene

pathetic fallacy the presentation of objects and events in nature as having human emotions and traits. These descriptions are often selected to reflect the actions and emotions of characters

pathos a scene or passage in a text designed to provoke sorrow or pity in the reader

personification an inanimate object or abstract concept is given human attributes or feelings

precipitating incident the event or action that sets the whole plot in motion

prophetic foretelling or foreseeing events, often through supernatural means

protagonist the main character in a story, poem or play

pseudonym a made-up or fake name, often used by writers to hide their identity

resolution the conclusion or ending when all the plot elements are resolved

reversal the development or change in a character is stopped or even goes backwards

rising action the plot and action develop towards the climax

sentimental, over-sentimental to be focused on emotional or tender feelings, and affected by feeling rather than thought or reason

simile two seemingly different things are compared to allow greater understanding of one of them. The words 'like' or 'as' are often used

sub-plot a secondary story, or plot, that runs through the main story

symbol, symbolise a sign that represents something else

tone the way the narrator speaks to the reader or a character speaks to another. Tone can also be set through description

Checkpoint 1 Scrooge seems mean and selfish. He only cares about gaining money for himself and doesn't care about others or what they think of him.

Checkpoint 2 Yes, we start to realise why Scrooge puts so much energy into obtaining money when we see his unhappy childhood.

Checkpoint 3 It represents the future, which is unknown.

Checkpoint 4 He hopes to make a connection and establish a relationship with the reader. This approach makes us warm to the narrator.

Checkpoint 5 It tells us Scrooge is a mean and harsh employer. It also tells us that Cratchit must be desperate for the job to put up with such treatment.

Checkpoint 6 We are meant to agree with the Charity Collectors' view. We have already been shown Scrooge is a mean person, so we are ready to reject his ideas.

Checkpoint 7 The fact so many different people are getting ready for Christmas emphasises the fact Scrooge is alone in his rejection of it.

Checkpoint 8 It emphasises how different these men are. We see that Cratchit is fun-loving despite being poor. Scrooge doesn't change anything about his routine, refusing to accommodate Christmas.

Checkpoint 9 This builds up the suspense and mystery, adding to the shock when the supernatural event happens.

Checkpoint 10 No, the fact he looks behind the door and has to verbally reject the sight shows he has been affected by it.

Checkpoint 11 To slowly build up tension and suspense. It makes us wonder what will happen at the top.

Checkpoint 12 To try and pretend he is not scared.

Checkpoint 13 This emphasises the fact Marley is no longer human.

Checkpoint 14 He breaks his normal routine, checking the door and verbally dismissing the events. This is similar to his behaviour after seeing the door knocker.

Checkpoint 15 This is similar to the detailed descriptions of the door knocker and the walk upstairs. It raises tension and suspense. The fact it is the church bell also reminds us that Scrooge will be judged after death; this is the same church bell that 'peeped slyly' at him on his way home.

Checkpoint 16 It is an old child. It represents a child who was young a long time ago.

Checkpoint 17 It suggests that the countryside is a happier place in which to live. The city is full of polluting industry, poverty and unhappiness.

Checkpoint 18 We feel sorry for Scrooge because he is upset. It also shows he does have humanity and emotion in him still.

CHECKPOINT 19 Fezziwig shows us that Scrooge did have happy times in his life. He also shows us how Scrooge should behave to Cratchit and his family. In addition this scene reminds us and Scrooge how badly Scrooge behaved at the beginning of the novella.

CHECKPOINT 20 The hat represents all the negative emotions Scrooge has collected since he was an innocent child. He pulls it over the Ghost to make the Ghost disappear because he cannot cope with the memories of what he once was. Memories can be with you forever. Scrooge's memories will only go if he forces them to.

CHECKPOINT 21 Scrooge has changed, but he does not yet realise the full implications of his behaviour. Although he knows he has behaved badly he has not yet been shocked enough to make the change permanent.

CHECKPOINT 22 It is the total opposite to Scrooge's lifestyle. Instead of pitying the Cratchits for their poverty, we admire their energy and commitment to each other as a family.

CHECKPOINT 23 This Ghost represents the future which is unknown. Therefore we cannot see what it looks like and it does not speak. It is far more sinister.

CHECKPOINT 24 They are poor and desperate. They have reached a stage when they only think of themselves and don't care about others. Dickens suggests

poverty creates criminals. Furthermore, Scrooge was so disliked they do not feel bad about stealing from him.

CHECKPOINT 25 It shows the harsh reality of his actions. Scrooge had not realised exactly what his current behaviour could lead to, and as he had already decided to change he wasn't expecting the name to be his. When he sees his name there he realises he was the dead man. It is the final push he needs to change forever.

CHECKPOINT 26 The weather has completely transformed. Instead of ice and snow there is sun and fresh air. It reflects Scrooge's change from a mean old man to someone who cares about others and does what he can to make their lives better. He has also found happiness in himself now.

CHECKPOINT 27 It emphasises the change in Scrooge and makes us take notice of how great the day is.

CHECKPOINT 28 Dickens' message is given in the Preface: he wants to outline some ideas about looking out for others. He hopes these ideas will stay with us and we will act on them.

CHECKPOINT 29 He does not have a job or enough money to spend on activities during the day so has to make the time go as cheaply as possible. He is not allowed to stay in his room, so has to go out.

CHECKPOINT 30 It is a time when families get together and people enjoy each other's company. He has no family and so this time makes life even harder to bear.

CHECKPOINT 31 Michael seems very meek and passive.

CHECKPOINT 32 No, but Michael cannot argue if he wants to keep the room. Dickens shows how poor people have very little power and have to make do with what they can find.

CHECKPOINT 33 They might be feeling guilty and uncomfortable about what they are hearing. They might realise that they have the ability to make Michael's life easier.

CHECKPOINT 34 He is a mean man who only cares about his money. He thinks Christiana only wants to marry Michael because she expects Michael to inherit all Uncle Chill's money when he dies.

CHECKPOINT 35 It shows us the great difference between what could have been and what is.

CHECKPOINT 36 Michael needs a safe haven to retreat to when life becomes unbearable. This is especially true around Christmas time.

CHECKPOINT 37 He seems competent, reliable and careful. He does not seem like the sort of person to imagine seeing ghosts.

CHECKPOINT 38 It helps to create the perfect setting for a ghost story. It reminds us of death and mystery.

CHECKPOINT 39 He appears to be a very nervy, jumpy man. He does not behave logically.

CHECKPOINT 40 The ghostly ringing is more of a vibration than a physical sound.

TEST YOURSELF

A CHRISTMAS CAROL

1 Scrooge *(Stave 1)*

2 Marley's Ghost *(Stave 1)*

3 The Ghost of Christmas Past *(Stave 2)*

4 Fred *(Stave 3)*

5 Scrooge *(Stave 5)*

6 Mrs Cratchit *(Stave 3)*

7 Ignorance *(Stave 3)*

8 Scrooge *(Stave 5)*

'THE POOR RELATION'S STORY'

1 Michael *(p. 116)*

2 Michael *(p. 117)*

3 John Spatter *(p. 123)*

4 Little Frank *(p. 116)*

5 Uncle Chill *(p. 118)*

6 Michael *(p. 120)*

'THE SIGNALMAN'

1 The narrator *(p. 105)*

2 The Signalman *(p. 110)*

3 Tom, the train driver *(p. 118)*

4 The Signalman *(p. 108)*

5 The Signalman *(p. 115)*

6 The Signalman *(p. 117)*

NOTES

NOTES

Maya Angelou
I Know Why the Caged Bird Sings

Jane Austen
Pride and Prejudice

Alan Ayckbourn
Absent Friends

Elizabeth Barrett Browning
Selected Poems

Robert Bolt
A Man for All Seasons

Harold Brighouse
Hobson's Choice

Charlotte Brontë
Jane Eyre

Emily Brontë
Wuthering Heights

Brian Clark
Whose Life is it Anyway?

Robert Cormier
Heroes

Shelagh Delaney
A Taste of Honey

Charles Dickens
David Copperfield
Great Expectations
Hard Times
Oliver Twist
Selected Stories

Roddy Doyle
Paddy Clarke Ha Ha Ha

George Eliot
Silas Marner
The Mill on the Floss

Anne Frank
The Diary of a Young Girl

William Golding
Lord of the Flies

Oliver Goldsmith
She Stoops to Conquer

Willis Hall
The Long and the Short and the Tall

Thomas Hardy
Far from the Madding Crowd
The Mayor of Casterbridge
Tess of the d'Urbervilles
The Withered Arm and other Wessex Tales

L. P. Hartley
The Go-Between

Seamus Heaney
Selected Poems

Susan Hill
I'm the King of the Castle

Barry Hines
A Kestrel for a Knave

Louise Lawrence
Children of the Dust

Harper Lee
To Kill a Mockingbird

Laurie Lee
Cider with Rosie

Arthur Miller
The Crucible
A View from the Bridge

Robert O'Brien
Z for Zachariah

Frank O'Connor
My Oedipus Complex and Other Stories

George Orwell
Animal Farm

J. B. Priestley
An Inspector Calls
When We Are Married

Willy Russell
Educating Rita
Our Day Out

J. D. Salinger
The Catcher in the Rye

William Shakespeare
Henry IV Part I
Henry V
Julius Caesar
Macbeth
The Merchant of Venice
A Midsummer Night's Dream
Much Ado About Nothing
Romeo and Juliet
The Tempest
Twelfth Night

George Bernard Shaw
Pygmalion

Mary Shelley
Frankenstein

R. C. Sherriff
Journey's End

Rukshana Smith
Salt on the snow

John Steinbeck
Of Mice and Men

Robert Louis Stevenson
Dr Jekyll and Mr Hyde

Jonathan Swift
Gulliver's Travels

Robert Swindells
Daz 4 Zoe

Mildred D. Taylor
Roll of Thunder, Hear My Cry

Mark Twain
Huckleberry Finn

James Watson
Talking in Whispers

Edith Wharton
Ethan Frome

William Wordsworth
Selected Poems

A Choice of Poets

Mystery Stories of the Nineteenth Century including The Signalman

Nineteenth Century Short Stories

Poetry of the First World War

Six Women Poets

For the AQA Anthology:
Duffy and Armitage & Pre-1914 Poetry

Heaney and Clarke & Pre-1914 Poetry

Poems from Different Cultures

Margaret Atwood
Cat's Eye
The Handmaid's Tale

Jane Austen
Emma
Mansfield Park
Persuasion
Pride and Prejudice
Sense and Sensibility

William Blake
Songs of Innocence and of Experience

Charlotte Brontë
Jane Eyre
Villette

Emily Brontë
Wuthering Heights

Angela Carter
Nights at the Circus
Wise Children

Geoffrey Chaucer
The Franklin's Prologue and Tale
The Merchant's Prologue and Tale
The Miller's Prologue and Tale
The Prologue to the Canterbury Tales
The Wife of Bath's Prologue and Tale

Samuel Coleridge
Selected Poems

Joseph Conrad
Heart of Darkness

Daniel Defoe
Moll Flanders

Charles Dickens
Bleak House
Great Expectations
Hard Times

Emily Dickinson
Selected Poems

John Donne
Selected Poems

Carol Ann Duffy
Selected Poems

George Eliot
Middlemarch
The Mill on the Floss

T. S. Eliot
Selected Poems
The Waste Land

F. Scott Fitzgerald
The Great Gatsby

E. M. Forster
A Passage to India

Charles Frazier
Cold Mountain

Brian Friel
Making History
Translations

William Golding
The Spire

Thomas Hardy
Jude the Obscure
The Mayor of Casterbridge
The Return of the Native
Selected Poems
Tess of the d'Urbervilles

Seamus Heaney
Selected Poems from 'Opened Ground'

Nathaniel Hawthorne
The Scarlet Letter

Homer
The Iliad
The Odyssey

Aldous Huxley
Brave New World

Kazuo Ishiguro
The Remains of the Day

Ben Jonson
The Alchemist

James Joyce
Dubliners

John Keats
Selected Poems

Philip Larkin
The Whitsun Weddings and Selected Poems

Ian McEwan
Atonement

Christopher Marlowe
Doctor Faustus
Edward II

Arthur Miller
Death of a Salesman

John Milton
Paradise Lost Books I & II

Toni Morrison
Beloved

George Orwell
Nineteen Eighty-Four

Sylvia Plath
Selected Poems

Alexander Pope
Rape of the Lock & Selected Poems

William Shakespeare
Antony and Cleopatra
As You Like It
Hamlet
Henry IV Part I
King Lear
Macbeth
Measure for Measure
The Merchant of Venice
A Midsummer Night's Dream
Much Ado About Nothing
Othello
Richard II
Richard III
Romeo and Juliet
The Taming of the Shrew
The Tempest
Twelfth Night
The Winter's Tale

George Bernard Shaw
Saint Joan

Mary Shelley
Frankenstein

Bram Stoker
Dracula

Jonathan Swift
Gulliver's Travels and A Modest Proposal

Alfred Tennyson
Selected Poems

Alice Walker
The Color Purple

Oscar Wilde
The Importance of Being Earnest

Tennessee Williams
A Streetcar Named Desire
The Glass Menagerie

Jeanette Winterson
Oranges Are the Only Fruit

John Webster
The Duchess of Malfi

Virginia Woolf
To the Lighthouse

William Wordsworth
The Prelude and Selected Poems

W. B. Yeats
Selected Poems

Metaphysical Poets